With best
and ' augun '

[handwritten signature]

MILESTONES

A Development

~

by

Lewis Hill

authorHOUSE®

AuthorHouse™ UK Ltd.
500 Avebury Boulevard
Central Milton Keynes, MK9 2BE
www.authorhouse.co.uk
Phone: 08001974150

First published by AuthorHouse 6/15/2007

ISBN: 978-1-4259-9939-1 (sc)

Printed in the United States of America
Bloomington, Indiana

This book is printed on acid-free paper.

Preface

For our mother Carmela Concetta Hill (née Sciuto-Sturzo)
Born 26:11:24 + died 30:6:05

La mamma Roma

3/7/05

La Mama Roma è eterna
La mamma Roma sarà
Domani come era ieri

Oggi la mamma Roma è quieta
Sotto il cielo azurro
Tranquillo senza perturbo
La mamma Roma beata
Conosce tutto,sappià tutto
Perdona tutto...

Ringraziamo Gesù Cristo
Per la vita
Della Mamma Roma
Città Eterna...

Acknowledgements

To my lovely wife Fiona and two wonderful children Adam and Rebecca

To my own family of brothers and sisters and to my Dad (still an Arsenal supporter after all these years!)

To all teachers including Andie Hudson who provided all the photographs & some of the drawings contained within this collection (and whose spirit and influence have moulded and shaped this couple of years).

Alison and Justin (as always): Good Luck

Walter and Bee who tolerated my sense of humour (occasionally)

All my friends and neighbours and fellow parishioners: may God bless you and keep you safe (but buy the book .)

All at AuthorHouse   thank you

CONTENTS

FAMILY

~

Nescio Quaerere

Luigi Collina
June 2006
Chelsea Physic Garden

I know not of what I speak
-Nescio quaerere- I know not of what I seek
I know only of that first long week
Wherein I didst discover mine own soul unique
How do I explain this without becoming quite oblique?
I thank the Lord for all his grace
That I should have joined the Human Race!

A Poet's Lament

LH 95

So this is the Pits-
Hanger Poetry Society
And what have we done?
I thought there was no such thing
As a Good Poet
Who didn't know Wit
But only a dead Poet
Who knew where to sit:
Amidst the talent
And the restless spirit
Wondering where the sixties went.

Now I need to sing,sing,sing,
Remembering the serious 'Hanging Judge'
a.k.a.Lord Jeffries of that Silk
(Aint that a funny thing)
Who no doubt over Lunch one day
May decline to hang my pictures at th'R.A.
Between a Tissot or van Gogh or some or other Manet
Where Monet Makes the whirled go round
The galleries, galleries, galleries...

So I write this little verse
With lines I yet needs rehearse
And though having rhymed wrong
Which with these words have made a fudge
I trust you don't judge so strong...

Pairing Hanger with Anger
And pits with King Coal
You might listen to this song
And deepest need to express a Muse
(debased by the acid rain of daily news)
You might just listen to my views
All bad poetry excuse
And
Herein hear my reason
Through this wet and wintry season...

My legacy if such there be
Is tenuous (if indeed I'm free):
To voice the feelings of some folks like me.

(Lifewish)

C 1994/1995

Spikenard-narrow up this stone edge path;
'Concentrate Caprione: it's a long way down'.
"Thirty thousand once strove along that plain
But boulders from mountain high struck down
The mighty warriors, unchastened by a howl of wind
As young men cried their last
                              (engouged upon a glint of blade)"
" yonder woods have stitched a cover for those remains
Whose soulful selfless voice they long preserve"

'No syzygy now that first winters's early storm is done.
Push higher little pup on yonder ridge
                              Whilst lost against the wind'.
The lie of battle over, climb higher 'gainst the setting sun
Steppe aside and look around: there lies young Hercules
Struck through by blade in heat of noise.
And awesome Lystra still bears the marks of scars long lost
To rotting time as earth his home dost make ;
And here lies little Sosthenes wherein he gave his life in vain
As he held that pass against the vandal.
And even as the leaf mould climbs ever higher still to settle
On some unknown ledge a dawn breaks
Against a psalm of bird-song

Sing sweet song of Nature
In shades of Resurrection

Covenant

July 1997
(minor amendments 2006)

When light ascends across the sky
      And cloud bursts open up to here
            While rain will penetrate the misty lie
And Nature's Law transcends the spear
      Of life and love from up on high
            This sunrise onto wild blue desolation
Opens onto hope of peace
      (some bloodied rainbow splintered insight lost)
      Emergent from the cloud gash at some grey real cost,
Where bleeding light points clearly to this earth,
      At birth within this cloud gap ruptured without mirth....
            Or fear of man marooned and moored alone on
            here without projection
All innocent of memory or connection...
      And still yet more of truth in reconciliation...

In long long Egyptian flight from clustered Pharoes kingdom banned
In Hebridean overture heavy with expectation, a rainbow like an open page
Turning in the wind of understanding and unbroken light
Appeared to reflect a path of light
(The self same wound now healing in good time)
This orange ray of sunburst, brother to the wind,
Is seen and prayed for like the autumn fruits of harvest;

Its sister rainbow, green and many coloured as a coat
Is heard deep in the heart stirring within prayer
And hoped for even through an anarche of despair
Together to be witnessed at one and same

Is then to believe in miracles and still be sane ....

Notes 2a good mother

you are the faithful bearer
of your angel spirits
borne in paine and love
manifest in this world and real...

Now you speak to all and any hearer

(able or unable to be heard)

From sun worshippers on holidays
         in Ibiza or Biarritz
To Denmark Hill and denizens of the
         'Son and Dove'
Even Christians on holy days and high days
         Keeping to their inner prayer wheel,
You are both adam and eve (and the apple)
and genesis and revelation

Good Luck and Good Knight

May I say thank you and sorry?

In the Park, December 2005
(just before Christmas)

By the banks of the River Brent 21/12/05

In the chill wind that blows through autumnal shades
The wide eyed silver grey glows from within the cloudy glades:
A feeling of expectant portent,
 A Massive Trans-illuminate from above,
            so that even the dulled earth looks upward
For inspiration from on high,
From our parents when we were young
The solid earth under a glowing vault
Aspires to better, higher things
As if gravity and dark earth have now released us
And like sparks we fly up from Job's cold fire.
We persevere, to hear the leaves'
Autumnal shades which my children
                Sigh and kick through as they play...

Perception

c.1999

Shadows long, Eden bright what need words that bite
East of Eden, Adam's slip
    Man borne of woman from the hip
Wave crest cusp, inchoate without, wordless within.
How can Adam conceive of sin if not without words within?
Five o'clock sheep dip time
In Mediterranean azure cool

After the Afrikaans like 'Bu Phasa' baptism
      Sun fire dried
Prior to the mass migration to the feeding lands of the enclosure
Later at evening meal at seven the finest view of Sicily with the wine...

Before all the bread unleavened this side of Etna withers in the evening sun
There but goes Adam, six, without one feeling of concupiscence, Innocent,
Full of Grace (of Childhood its own Sacrament)
Unaware of sin as unaware of Law
As of waiting within for Perception's Door
To open out to us, to let his parents in
To Adam's world...and let their spirits like the angels soar...

My Little Girl

Girl, as in "Perception's" boy before
Wills herself around
While daddy opens doors
She walks right through them without a sound
Epicycle 'pon epicycle
Near the epicentre of Dante's purgatory
And not too far in tantrums from lava territory
Angel dust pure and just a proper little angel
She wills her way away around any obstacle
Sometimes moving sideways like a farmers coracle
Pierced and pained this anguish of Happiness remembered
(the greater torment of Happiness forgotten)
She plays with friends Billy and Huey
And falls asleep tired as a doll
Self composed as any New York moll
Because she knows (like Adam when he slips a funny joke)
This daddy's just a silly 'bongy' head
Who doesn't make his own bed...
Unless each slow breakfast morsel
Is to him to be fed
At his last, in his dotage
Like King Lear nursing his damaged cochlear...

Victory,
Angel.
Sculpture
V.A.
by John Flaxma
-Koo..

5.1.03
Loupan
Vi

14

Now We Are Five or Six or 7-Up

Summer 98 (with acknowledgements to T. Pertenue)

Winstone the Smelly
Tigre (and ETHIOPE)
Tanga and Low
Rabbit (Welsh or myxomatosed)

Had an adventure (care of legal indenture)
And using Christoph's Gin and Ribena
Ee-yaws,
Ee-yaws,
Ee-yaws
All the way home
As from closing time
 they wander and roam...

Bending Light Round Gravity's Rainbow
(Brehmstrahlung Radiation)

March 1998

At the zoo pushing the chair
Not thinking heavy thoughts re:in CARNATION
Or other non allergenic diaried dairy products....
Or counting out my life in coffee spoons and formula powder for his sister...

After the coypus in the rain and the white parakeet on a stand
After the piranhas and the big fish and the alligator
After the talk and the noise
In the rain my five year old son said 'I lost my life'
As if in the midst of all this Zoo Life there appears
                    A Loving Echo from some-ones' previous memory
Some former history some previous Life in premature conclusion
That my five year old was voicing without knowing
'Where did you last see it?' I quipped unthinkingly
'In the rain' replied the guileless devastation of the innocent, in inner sense
'It's blowing away in the rain'
'Just blowing in the wind...'
Yet when I write this phrase on the white lined paper of this book
There is no limit to the bone crunching punch behind this simple phrase
All I could say after that hiatus was:
Can I put that into a poem,young AdamAnt
(up and at'em,boy)
In order to rediscover
this heaven sent earthly joy.

Sicilian Holiday 1999

Mind how the Sun's elemental Nature
Will raise you up to slowly teach ya
And as your mood warms up in stature
You turn around, another 'pollo arrostito'
On the sandy shore, feet unshod by the poolside
Dousing yourself Cajun style in cream
Soaking away in a bath of petty pain
Dipping your toes (Heaven knows)
In the washing stones of standing imperception
Not daring to stare the sun straight in the eye
Lest, Prometheus burnt, we wrestle with the chains which bind
Humanity to its elemental mountainside
Falling like Icarus, angel wings clipped
Into an anguished Etnean gaping gash
Smouldering in the boulder bound heat
Blinding us even as we fall and burn and see our waxen wings dissolved...

Family

Late 1996 /Early 1997

I bid you good night
My day is long and I am short
Of energy.
I bid you good night
     That I may sleep
            In flight
Of dream and somnolence and camel hair
I bid you good night
    That I may join my
                    tired family upstairs
As soon as I have prepared my youngest's
                      milk
I bid you good night
         In a formula of assent and silk
That I may sing God's praises 'ere
               I sleep
Lest the morning find me without comfort
             Torn from Life to the hereinafter
             by some knowledge
                of this world's affairs...

Needs Must Write

(When the devil drives to work)

5-03-07
First Monday after the March moon Eclipse 2007

A mother and her daughter
And a daughter as her mother
(As above then so below)
Of spirit good, strong hearted full and true
Both in faith hold onto their journeys' bus handles of Life
On time's long journey in good times and in strife
Both in need of golden rays from golden healing sun
Like flowers drinking in the soft, soft rain of winter introspection...

Amidst the fearful echo of *abandon*
In a week-end witness to Nature's deepest awesome numinosity
Well remembered is knowledge that we are fragile on this speck of earth
In the infinite solitude and abundant silence of universe's long dark night
We cling to rock as we do to ourselves and also others
Like flowerers in the rain awaiting Apollo's healing rays
That they are close and harmonied yet somehow insistent counterpoint
Remains that though distinct their oneness is their difference:
That they cannot get yet closer
They feel they are 'apart'
But of their nature and their universe they are a part...

As above so below: mother daughter, daughter mother
Each a person unto the other
AND yet please God once they sleep God's balm

That they be resourced and at peace
Reminds us all that of their spirit they have a lease
And please God let them know
That who they are is more than just a show
And once the evening settles down
Amidst the rain and winter glow
Of firesides and hugs and tea
Their spirit and inner source the most worshipfull a God
Of Loving worship still may light the darkness
Dissolve the dinginess of constraint

And bring in that aspect most complete
The love of self, the love of God, the loving others
Their mysteries to foretell, their histories and their lives well spent
In divine contemplation. Even as the gravity of the moods that we imagine
Bends the strait lined arrow
Through a curvature of Social space-time Caused
By an innate sorrow both tomorrow and today that we should borrow,
That we should borrow, the metaphor of our moon's perceived eclipse
Distorted slung-shot light-bolt by gravity is ellipsed...
Which presence alters images even that that caused
Our curved earth's even greater curved shadowy 'orizon.
That we perceive the really real
We interpret through our sleep filled night and clarion call to dreams
That human dreams by angels wings and golden Morpheus' golden dust
Be nightly touched by Magick to resource our Perception's morrowed day

Each soul its own gravity will bear
That by its heaviness draws in near
Our only God's divine understanding loving light to hear
That yet though none of us be philosophy's '*ubermenschen*' dear
We may somehow still absolve humanity and be of conscience clear...
Yet touched by light from god head bright
We can and do say that *I love you* phrase because Once when I was so young
I heard my own parent - god say 'I love you' to this writhing louse in
        their own voice.
My god-light and his passion and compassion did soon follow
And enough a day to laugh out loud (and to build for Comedy a healing house)
That we can say 'we care', *j'espere*, that we remember well
Arriving into heaven from out this hell
And care we do (because others show us that they did do too ...)

I do not know why I must write, my Muse
Just to be in mind that I should forsooth a Muse amuse...
That of this awful rhyming please *je m'accuse* and please excuse
For each and ev'ry moment that a daughter to her mother
And *her* mother to *her* daughter
We reflect (*none methinks their feet do wash in soda water*)
That we needs must sleep that we also needs must dream in peace and
        happiness *serene*
And so *as above then so below*
The simplest of harmonies now disturbed

Like rippling waters at Bethesda's healing angel pool
A caring spirit most perturbed

Lights a candle (*'Praise to God her Source'*)
Remembering that sleep is its own sublime virtue
Most divine as humanity to its heaven a head inclines,
And in Loving kindness loves her daughter as *herself...*
And more besides. As God's own sweetest sucre
                    the Source of that One's Life...(Again)

Blessed be to Mary Bee
That heaven's angels we shouldst see
As sovereign on this earth but privy to our own distanced Heaven's Birth

EDUCATION...
EDUCATIONEDUCATION...
EDUCATION...

~

Memory

1995(amended)

Something always
(Never yesterday's
Unfinished business?)
Haunts the churches still
Quiet as a storm lashes
The Saints in their transparency
Letting a fine line of dusted light
Touch gently the Kiss
Up on the Altar

And I look, watching, broken
In a pew at the back of the Church-
Apse, reflected on the ether ripples
Of the baptismal font observed
On the patterned ceiling overhead.

Air, Water, Fire and Earth
(Ozone, Ice-Caps, Holocaust and the Remains of the Day)

All Saints Day 2005

When the Easter melody becomes an air
And graces us with tomorrow's world and heirs
When the Mediterranean and Caspian seas before the Flood
Become as one and naturally as Christ to Blood
Will flow more sweetly than wine and snow to water,
Might like a childhood game extinguish th'eternal flame
Inebriating the family with love of sons and daughters
In Eden each of everything can be gi'en a name
To put it in its place amidst the myriad stellar plane
From the "Inns of Court" to
    "Cheshire Cheese" and "Wig and Pen"
The history of Nagasaki and Hiroshima loom large
When now and then it seems we 'D'NAe ken'
'Cept that which we use to anaesthetise the pain,
While following the antics of Ben or Marge
On some midday cultural never ending
    drama as we should
Do we remember that life is for the Good
And not always just for Christmas even if writ large?

Medical School Lunch:
Greens With Duck a l'Orange

February 2005
(Name noted in Spring 1976)

Null cell specialist and 'Patience Strong'
Microscopist and the sober,
 The sound of mind and wind
And those right on the edge
Of discovery and excitement
The well-to-do and student pauper
Scraping the crumbs off the table
After the broth and roll;
The caring and the alienated,
The Honourables and the MPhil'
The bloke after Friday lectures at the Bar
 And those who relish the anatomy
 And of the black-biled melan-chole know some thing...
Those to whom menarche is a mystery
And those who know and value the ague
And rheumy joints of all our souls
Those whose experience reduces existence to the measurable
 Only to view life from the outside
And those whose only wish is to experience the spirit of physiology.
The 'rugger-buggers' of course were there listening in
And trying to dictate to their shorter fellows
The Cheltenham ladies college head girl
And the man from Malaysia
Learning the biochemistry of osteoporosis
The Old Wykehamist and the Old Harrovian
Sharing the round with the Old boy from Battersea Grammar;
 And the ones that you only notice after a term
That you have never seen before and after a while then you don't
All these and more cross across the college square
Norfolk Place London, home of the discovery of Penicillium notatum
As a by product of defence of its own Life
Which is always lauded to the heavens as the miracle of wonder drugs,
Medicine's Song of Songs.   Indeed it is. While it lasts...
While it belongs to that which we long to belong: Life
Just don't mention the unsung heroin behind that great Mann's magic mountain
Whoops! Derived from morphine as a safe alternative to Victorian laudanum
Another designer label FC-UK but Sworn on the Bible...to be
Witnessed by its commissioner for oaths...Without the Hope
Inherent in a black economy across the road at 'Fountains Abbey'

Doctor PainE, I presume

c.1999/2000
written within Rome while in the gift of my mother's spirit

From our summer residence of childhood memory
That one I associate to school summers
Away from Virgil and Agricola
Negative numbers, Animal classification
And of course Sunday on Sunday
Of Dickens: "Love's Labours Lost",
I look out on the changes to this small boy's eyes
From within, I remember the Sunday walk with *'nonna Giulia'*
To buy 'gelati con la panna'
Just to see the look on this small boy's face (which of course I couldn't)
And the flock of sheep being led along our road to the field by a shepherd
(Where another year a whole helicopter had to land for safety)
And which today thirty years on is a dual carriageway,
On the edge of this verdant sunken playground
There is the same landmark petrol station selling more 'Fina',
For a moment with my family I watched
Those cypress trees swaying as if on the Via Appia
In the wind of revelation and sudden shock.
I stand in communion with my sorrow
For having studied Anatomy, Pathology and Gynaecology
In place of Latin, French and Greek...

And for a moment I held my breath in the midday sun
Over the Via Flaminia, running south.

To think that this was once my holy of holies in my innocence

My New Jerusalem for which I now weep
My childhood estate separate from me by a toyshop of broken glass
As if I can watch but not play,
Pray but not keep watch in the midnight garden of Gethsemane
And so my own son asks me for food and in due course I resume
My botanical observation of the imagined cypress trees of old,
(Trees which you smell long before you see or hear them in the wind)
Holding in their sway huge swathes of washed white silk

I do not weep for Mediterranean blue skies, which cloudless,
hold the secret of Eternity
I do not cry at my incompetence and 'missed off' opportunities
Constituting one more sophisticated intrusion into mine own 'zeitgeist'

I weep for the separation from my hopes and prayers
And in my confusion and anger my lost serenity,
this Italian heritage and my Englishness,
my songs, my love of an Oxford alumna ,
and my memory of med school
and ...this lost inner sense...

I reflect on my incognate acceptance into the Terra Romana
A filmic dissonance washing its hands of all our humanities

Even as the surgeon prepares for operation, stitching shut an open wound
Caused by too much knowledge of the world's affairs...
Too much knowledge of the world aware
This sadness at lost innocents shot through by aims at high 'intentions'
This ironic catholic nature falling flat on foreign ears
Suggesting solutions 'stead of horror at experiments without pardon...
This soul looks out over the Garden of Gethsemane, Rome
This 'Akeldama' so quickly stopped and checked in place
This feeling of lost hope made good by swaying trees
Drunk with the historic present known to Cicero et alter

Drives me to my pen to write some words and phrases

That when I wake from dream
Though I will die, it will be not yet.
And though I feel the cold dark glass of separation
(even if now filled with Irish stout)
It will only be what doctors call the Pane Syndrome
For which if I may I thank the Lord.

Srebrenica

Circa 1998 / 1999

There is a corner of this little England
That is forever foreign,
There is some corner of a sceptred isle
That will be forever so forgot
There is a corner of this little England
That will be forever foreign,

There seems no end of insularity
Between the Isle of Dogs and Barking
(Across the road from Charon lives our 'Trace')...
Should you let it slip that you are catholic (even in your haste)
In some forgotten corner of this sceptred realm
You might soon enough be forgotten
Along the lonely paths
That only church mice chew...

Ealing Hospital Paradigm Shift

2006

Paradigm shift? What paradigm shift?
At the hospital in X ray by the lift
A heavy cast released a weighty spirit
Entombed and mummified, a dead poet's ghost hand you might intuit
X rayed beyond today back to yesterday once more
While dolly on a trolley sleeping deeply cries not snores
Asking for some water in delirium, febrile, and unwell
Science, knowledge or profession or to others another heaven from another hell
My son's nurse scrapes the plastered saint
 From off his hand: (whilst ward, dilapidated, flaky paint,)
Asking of the miracle for both Adam G and Adam H, both 'query scaphoids'
Both healed by time and nature's registrar (consultoid)
Supervising nature's farm ecology, all-healing Lex and Alms
While casting nowt on shadowed X- ray nor patient's supine health.

Where Once was Eden
(now we sit to watch the workmen build)

Easter 2005

In Elysian green, we walked the path
Treading underfoot no camomile, no smile
'Pon our faces: (we knew too well the aftermath
Of cold showers remembered in our thoughts
And therefore present with us for a while).
As we dreamt of hope under the starlit cloudless sky,

We hoped that tomorrow would be a glimpse of heaven too
Where we might petition THAT which is unnameable
To hear our pleading and pathetic nature, our humanity
Without the yeast of culture
(for here on earth our bread's unleavened)
We do not entertain that we are not capable
Of understanding the divine nor yet of prayers appearing to remain unanswered.
For to be with rivals, friends or enemies maintains our sanity.
But that was yesterday, and this, today.

To have been pushed through this Life is not to ask for why
Is not to be of mind to have your say
It is the part of the 'there and then': 'to do is to obey'
But this is now and that was then
Even as that phrase
        'all men die the only question when?'
Nags me still, tugging at me as an orphan child, demanding to be heard
For that which we dare not hope
(that we should see eternity in a grain of sand
And a moment, like the sea side postcard
        Filled with holiday,
In the infinity of an azure sea 'neath an azure sky)
Is not to be of mind to have a hope
Of pleading for our Humanity.
Walking on Elysian green is neither time present
Nor time imagined, neither true
Nor English- rather it is Greek, imported from an
        Oxford College.

But 'my' cypress trees along that 'Via Cassia' scene
                    From Our Italian balcony in Rome
Brings me here to smell that heady geranium bliss
Of Restaurant flowers watered in the evening sun
And brings her to smell that eternal 'time present' of a 'pelargonium
                    vitifolium' dripping wet and overhanging,
From which we build a house into a home
That becomes the spirit which subsumes
Us all –plus every generation from beyond the fall.

Εννὺς μὲν ἡ σὴ
περὶ παυτωη ληθη.
ἐννυς δε ἡ παυτων
περὶ σοῦ ληθη.

MARCUS AURELIUS

Human: ALL too Human

Sometimes when my mood is low
At conjugation of circadiana and so
 With new moon rising o'er an open field
Of thought, and Feeling
That earth's goodness in me won't allow
At spring time some sincerely held belief
Reflecting on the harvest of my soul, Fiona
To thank God for my son and daughter
Sprinkled with love and light like holy water
Thanking God for these loves that don't alter
Without which I would not be here
 But lying in some gutter looking up at stars
Counting not my blessings but my scars...

I would not be here, but whitened lips
Be Lying face down, inert, insensitive, immune
Unnoticed at the bottom of a pool, this fool
Whose, life unrealised,
(whose talent un-promised was therefore undelivered
Like the Pizza from the Restaurant at World's End
Or Universe Beginning...)
Might be as always
...'Politic , cautious , no doubt an easy tool'...
Without Times' Promethean winged chariot hurrying near
Still queuing for Wessex County tales' 'Ficciones'
Or other legal fiction in contradiction to Belief
 Might enter this next life unfinished , if un-forgiven
Like Phlebas (Royal College Phoenician this fortnight dead)
Entering indiscriminately the whirlpool
(that welcomes Arab, Gentile, Christian, Jew even Inuit too)

With only a prospect of Aurelian forgiveness
Inherent in the phrase

'a little while and my memories will be washed in the waters of
         forgetfulness
That little while more and my memory will be washed there too.'

to hold out some semblance of salvation
Even if not necessarily forgiveness
(for which I'm sorry in advance lest I forget an unseen purgatory to be)...
In some or other mystic realm reality...
Hoping to hear the holy forgiveness of Jesus' word
Cry out 'Abba, Father', at the Sermon on the Mount
(And at my last, I hope...)

'Blessed be those that mourn,
         for The Truth shall be their consolation'

God's plan for Job and Man: to seek salvation is to persevere
Especially when long night's mantle 'cross the human field draws near...
Do not go spirit 'Gentle'...but please stay here this tale to bear ...

Humane Gnomic Utterances Project

(Apologies for any 'Roget's Theosaurus'
 that slipped out the Jurassic Park
Electric ring-fence just
Like dark dinosaurs out of the subconscious)

The Door is locked
And the way is blocked
Mere anarchy is loosed
Upon 'Les Parisiennes' without excuse
Overhead and overheard
That saviours starlight
Appears too soon a search light
Shone out upon the herd
To spy on yonder midnight fight,

To fly on yonder mingled flight...

The door is locked
And the way is blocked
How oft has this been said
There is no other way (alive or dead)
And so these feelings like a flock of folk
Accumulate to silt my veins
'neath this tattered battered barren cloak...

The door is locked
The way is blocked

A 'not at home' sign hangs undisturb'd
This lunch time the cross borne expert is not here

The door is locked
          Someone's thrown away the key
(nor did I know that it keeps me in ,
With attention and self care
Not out, without infinity to bind its cure
This side of sanity: beyond it is mere anarche'
And the bloodied martyrs' testimonials)

The door is locked
And the way now blocked
And searchlights overhead.
 Distant rumbling blades unheard:

A lost dystopic inner vision
Where 'far away is close at hand,
 In images of elsewhere'
Emblazoned across any cold, cold call
Cold played television screen...
The door is locked
And the way is blocked
But daylight life will soon appear
To open up to morning's daily start...
Along the Rue d'Orsay
'Orseaux' we're told (and other schoolboy jokes of old)

The door is locked as is my heart
So my daughter why do I weep so?
Is my door shut fast as well
And I do not hug and do not hear
Does my face look not as heaven so much as hell?
Helas! This searching light appears
Throughout my heaviness not so to illuminate my fears
As to discretely prophet from them all,
As they are herded, one by one,
Eyes wide shut in dreamland,
And gassed in tears and laughter
And kept in cheque to keep the peace...

Everybody passte their Spellynge teste 'Cept lyttle Geoffroy Chaucerre

In memory of my uncle Robert Gloucester Hill
born 7/3/21 died 14/7/2003 in Brecon

Robert Graves on a Welsh hylsid spellbound
by th'eternal imagery, (of his Whyte Goddesse),
Buried in those earthworkes (hero-soldier here entombed):
No Valhalla nor cremation nor baptismal fire?

Merely our hearts burning
within us, walking to Emmaus as we aspire)
Burning within some physiology
Bounden Promethean Lewis' Inflammation
Angry and on fire and on ice
yet still cool without desire
As we falle into the water
Though it was upwards that we aspired...

Upstairs, downstairs Mrs Bridges
May have confused Lady Morphia
With somebody who cared
For the ailing souls at life-end, scared
But for Florence Nightingale in the Light
And pain relieving head dress that she wore
Bidding health and wholeness to the now eternally serene...

With sanguine fervour producing for her starving hosts
Five Dreaming forms of sardine sarnies
                    and sups of ale at half their usual cost...
Of course,kept cool with her own sangfroid neigh *sang real*
Drawing down experienced voice from her own chosen inner cabal:
An inner hero's tale of Sang Real? sant Graal? Holy Grail?
Maybe Merovingian crossing of the scoring line

For an Arthurian game at Rosslyn Park and rugby 7s
-though I never really went -
To think back over bitter herbs and bread unleavened

Never really tried to score that goal (but was affected just the same)
Where was this mythological mystical other world ?
This nether heaven for a Middle Earth ?
This trans-illumination of all our souls ?
I wait for the passing shadow

Still desperately seeking the spirit of someone just so kind...
(Tennessee Williams' Desiree)...
Re-lying...
Am I being too Sanguine? Sung wine ?Or Something under mind
                    (At this graveside I certainly feel somehow undermined)...
White Goddess (unknown spirit of the wind)
Reminding me of my filial realty and duty to my own mind...
 Seeking out Rome's Eternal Vestal flame, its spirit un-extinguished...
No more subject to pagan atheroma (nor that o'er demanding insulinoma)
Some memory of soma and its psyche, animus and anima...
A house builded on foundation
And so to there (my own childhood memory) in this tired tardy telling
Becomes retolde where knights of olde had had their spirits re-emboldened

Like demi gods in their earth laboratory tending mice
In just one flick , the telling taile
Reveals the truth that set the spirit free...
The hopes of understanding yet to be ...

Chaucerre (pilgrimme passte) retold the Moral storie
 Pagan, Christian, Children's Tober morry
Doctor Foster, Doctor Spin, Jackanory
(Holding all to laws and childhood toys and transport Lorries)
Each their own with their own worries
All can heede from firste to laste
The web-like spell that has been caste...

(So when you do then don't bee sorrie
 If or when you finally reach 'Sartori')
 But wait and stop and look and listen
When you're moments from that heaven
To hear the welcome with you in the afterlife
                    of Some One Else's Glory ...

March 2006

Human Diversity :
Guardian Angel Dust

2005

From Aardvark to Zymurgy
(That A to Z of wrong spelling)
And post production drug testing
'A little bit of hard work never gave any one any arms'
(Unlike Reagan and his cohorts)
Thalidomide was not intended but by God was real
There was I made to realise that 'Christ was Victim'
As well as unsung hero of our undeserv`d grace,
From the NMR of the 'I love you'
At the *'Corpus Christi'* Public house
Where Publicans and Singers meet
To the Collapse of Supersymmetry
Which invokes that Nature's Force
Drawn as if by spirit to its mass
In all reality... the earth did move
As it spun around an orbit
Like a kiss that is broke winded
And pinned and plated to its mount,
 And tagged and acting through a distant Latin Mass
On some first Sunday of some quiet month
A gospel according to Lefebvre and a dogma,
 Which fever is yet unbroken if as yet unchecked,
To the Oenology and Viticulture of the Grape
 Pressed and bottled
'Premier Cuvee' to keep
Our souls in shape:

My God, nobody deserves to be a Victim...

Standing on our differences
Shooting at that moon
Childhood astronauts, would be footballers,
And other innocents yet unborne
Might in just a little while without our knowing
Turn,
And crown us with some thorns...

O God let us hope we grow,
Stronger and wiser before we lose that long preserved humanity that
        we call ours.
That we think we own.

So often have I felt so low: but not enough to harm
 My Self or any other...
 Yet suicide may not be painless after all...
Indeed might hurt like hell
'...Why do I hear this fear around and round
the fish bowl of my skull
Swimming like some two lost souls inside my brain,
 Year after year...'
Nor would I inflict this on a crowd without hope or cure
Yet like Pavlov I too can hear a bell when I must feed,

And dull
Thinking, only thoughts that others must seem endure.

From those that have a 'something'
                To those that have a not at all
Between the blues, the Purple,
                Lies the pink and the well read,

To the green and orange it's the best that's left unsaid
(for that *is* our lot and this
                The science of material and of silks)
Our unsung heroines guide us through some moral maze;
Along the memory strewn paths to the Memory
That casts its shadow that re-fuses
 To recall that dream last night that we are
Living a life that totters from... daze to daze...
Even entering the Grande Hall,
                Even speakynge unto Kings.

Voting with our feet from stashe`d arsenal at Highbury
To the hubris and hutzpah of Tottenham London N West
(Still could this be Tottenham Hotspur
Discovering The Arsenal at Highbury?):
This language I do not speak, and that the thing
Between the Christian and Easter this next year

(Is lamb with mint sauce or with rosemary?)
The broader we will build our phylacteries
The longer others write on them
                    Their double barrelled names
And point them on this first full day of that Fox Hunt
Looking like the more we get our defences in line first
(Crossing the road map to Peace to reach the other side
 Ask, are we leaving behind the intention to do Good?)
The more we un-block not just our competition

Guess what?
The more we un-block our own drains and brains
So that sans everything we no longer piss on our own boots,

By God, but Kiss the sacred Dove of Love
(as it deposits Thought within our Minds)

When we fear to spike the Villain's guns
 Do we then hand to him our keys ?
We really will be without help, forever so forlorn,
Remembering the Kiss of Peace Before Communion
And 'What the Thunder Said'
(The delicate sound of thunder)
In some far off Eastern wasteland
                    Within some pre- text of a union
As it journeyed o'er both th'alive and dead
Remembering that Peace that passeth Understanding...
And rememberings of remembrance of our own time's past...

But
As long as 'eggs' is 'x'
And day is day (by God it's long)
That Golden rule remains the same
And here's the 'why' and wherefore
' Do unto others as we are wont to be done unto'
 Even before one goes to work upon an EEG...
 As we ponder, post-Chernobyl, in this life, crying 'View Halloo'
As yours truly   falls off horse to end up black and blue...
Indeed yes my mother's life still within me lives
For that was my noble Song and this my noble steed
That taught me write from wrong
 That Alwaies needes we hope be stronge...

When I Dream, I Dream of Angels

2005

Once I held a dream within my hand
It was a fine dream made up of gossamer silk
Woven by the denizens of underground caves and huge canyons grand
It spun a film reality dew drop on dew drop of spider's milk;
It so engrossed me into enduring reality's second chance
Regurgitated at night re-chewed human circumstance
Finest dairy cream of life, and milk of human kindness,
That I willingly put away my childish things of day
To hold onto my night time ration of glorious wildness
Whilst all the time praying for my 'terrors' to be held at bay.

I swam through deepest of oceans of azure,
I climbed every mountain high their thinning atmosphere to endure
I even hunted wild animals corralling them into my holy ark
Drove steam engines and fast cars
Aimed rockets into the night sky's
Dark and Lovely 'ciel de nuit' to seek out the reality of stars...

Dreaming, dreaming, dreaming...
Later when I aspired to the archetypal dreaming spires
Of Wisdom, Influence Might, high above these desires
Seeking out my lost song mythology of Love,
I strove to climb tender academe's great height
But graduated, thank God,unto prayer unto the Holy Dove.

When next some human tragedy befell me (so I thought)
My dreams unrealised but dim and brought to nought
My REM collection though live unplugged and deeply hid
Where all but the bravest wanderer went
I did not need ought that was not 'heaven sent'
 So now and then to this comforted Job
Appears from my sloughed despair some wholeness unknown
 That reconciles the evil day
Through the power of the hidden cross into something that is good
Much less sense appeared in me than I hoped it would
But now with out the hope of remedy I pray
(Because That is where I am today)...

Unless the lovely Angel lead me up where will I find my path to light?
Unless the lovely Angel show me how
                    (when I spread my wings to follow her in flight)
How shall I gain entrance into that awesome sight that is our joyous
        heavens' realm?

Wide is the Gate-Control Theory of Pain

14.02.06

And I saw in heaven a throne as though of burnished bronze renown
And upon it a figure as that of a man and upon his head as it were a crown

And though I know that all good things to those who wait appear
There are times when the muse moves me not to say that which is not in my ear

Reflecting on 'the final common pathway' even the patricians of Queen Square
Neurologising and eulogising on how good the old theories were

Acknowledge as a college the mystery of the conscious
While sometimes washing their hands like good old Pontius

(To be thinking on higher things): on the human condition
For wide is the gate that leads to perdition
And long is the path
And hard is the math...
'Judgement difficult and experience fallacious'
And quite often science is wide of the mark but still highly contagious...

Money talks (unto Money): Love is Light
(and he ain't heavy)

September 2000 (amended 2002)

Whilst speaking to my bank one day I countered but did not specify
      my numbers sterling;
Great clouds of drifting feeling off the frenzied mud were all I could
      muster unprepared
Like a chlorine stench over an entrenchment of defence and monetary
      values shared.
This I could not contain as the foundation of my life yet
Cold with poverty grew, and rotten feet complained of wet .
Cluster shell after cluster shell appeared to devastate the settled ground,
Blasting into soil huge wheals of tortured dust Across a cratered
              moonlit 'scape and crust'
Aerating the poppy seeds of Consolation after torment .And mistrust
Coiled tight amidst the brackened enclave like a slave
Muddied and bloodied with no view to these Futures(or the reasons passed)
I sit listening intently to the noise and fury.
Another broadside from the heavy artillery of finance
Demanding immediate repayment on most uneasy terms
Firing from yonder hill: and 'look there is the morning sun'
So I scurry –broken winded- in the half light of breaking day across
      the defensive wire
Computer keyboard my only arsenal:(a weapon that is up
             and primed and used with skill- and summed sadness)
Ignoring all the mortal dangers to myself I *single handedly* secure
      th'attention
              of my foe and so...

I promise to repay the bearer on demand an interim repayment (if but slow)
Before the promised finance reinforcements show
Coming from behind our lines to substantiate the shell shocked weary troops
(taxed beyond endurance by the continual pounding of economic canon)
To make good the breech in our liquidity in groups
By the rising of this 'Sun of York'(at closing time and beyond)
To fill the air with drunken silence and the prospect of that peace this
      long good Friday,
That passeth understanding (and much else besides)...

Weighting for deliverance from th'invention of the un-lagged tank
Young Winston, (him of Brixton Hill), shivers and in his prime
Ministers to his folks, in silent grief,
      As his voice lives on, black vinyl in echoes brief,
Mouldering in the ditch water of attrition still,
While overhead the stock exchanged and fired works of war
Still whizz bang in the timed perfection of ballistics and artillery shells and hells
Flying through the memory of All our Yesterdays (and their sad, bad,
      mad, rehearsals)
And all the folks who long gone from here, in their dispersals
Pin their hopes like medals on the rails of white housed demi gogs;
I stop to listen to the spirit of Vietnam and Laos, Korea and this Last Test
Built up in many years of cagey unrest
And colder rhetoric yet, warmed upon South London's broken fires
      electric,heard
I stop a minute between the Medellin and Shanghai's Golden Crescent
To listen to the fragrant songbird sing of these my fears in this my present
To alight upon an icy, icy fire, a pool of blood a moment and a choir
Heard And so I say Amen Amen Our men. To what then should we aspire?
To th'invention of the light in all this heat this night?

A Kings' Appeal Has Been Lost (again)

c. 1986 LH

I
KING AHASUERUS :
His professional engagements are separate
                    From his social diary,
So soon discovered in lament
As one who is small, quiet and wiry.
II
MORDECAI in his polyester suit
Hates to hate but with violent skills
Shifts his view to make some loot
Able to accumulate sufficient unto his bills.
III
Today a growing concern occurs
When friends in conversation meet
An exchange of minds which spurs
Both One and two-faced Janus in to eat.
IV
At breakfast, lunch and supper,
Or at meal times at the Bar
DISCUSSING Politick ideals under happier
Climes, or which is the better car.
V
At long last Mordecai reaches,
For a warm Satsuma, dates and nuts
With whom or which he preaches
Conversion to this Clueless Klutz

The Contract
($200 that's the price on the streets
Jazz singer Satchmo declares)

Autumn 2005

'Man is borne free and everywhere he is in chains
What is the reason for this curious state of affairs?'
Opined Rousseau, philosopher in his 'Contrat Social'
He accumulates through his sins many a heavy pain
 Protecting himself and what he desires so this he cannot share.
That is the first link without which there would be no gaol
Without the punishment of deprivation there would be no fear
Without the loss of separation and lack of mail
There would not be pain nor fear of Sheol
Without this sanction the law and the cross would be empty
Without redress un-amended rights inevitably would do wrong
In that case that would be the second link
All this so far should stop and make us think
Should we not grow and show how we have become strong...
The third link in this chain grows slowly within our own time
And melds the gravity to our souls.
Wholesome and raised we carry our cross
And do not notice that we trip and fall...
Everywhere man is borne free
  But everywhere he is in chains
The reasons I have shown I cannot explain nor see
There is always the prospect of discovery
That we as mere humans might hear the Spirit 'Very':
"Che l'amore si trove nel vero cuore"

After visiting the Tolpuddle Martyrs Memorial, Dorset

The Bloodstone (from Estonia)

Circa 1995 (amended)

An image of weight embossed
By better hands than mine, with symbols
Of thought, might, our power,
Thrown in a lake (forever lost?)
Crossed keys of late(a moonstone Rhine stone)
Dropping 'spiritus mundi' onto incandescent plate
Changing traffic lights in a crossroads faraway
                                    (stuck on red)
A dark blood red moonstone – a rhinestone
Marked with a cross, hanging on a chain
Portrays the face peering in,
Sharp edged theatrical:
 A Stone to Cast Away Doubt Maybe?
A stone to die for (I don't think so)
Sincerely hope not
See the face always skilfully reflected in its colour
See the edge, the line of jaw, teeth, a smile flickering, electric,
Two sockets (closely set where the eyes should have it).
The shock of red (Jack Ruby red)
To recognise the skill and crossed bones
Of a pirate buccaneer (a very gem of history)
To light a Pilate light in your house
(praying the heating is still central)
And, starting to wash your hands of ethnic cleansing,
Crossing the Rubicon.

Blood Stone

circa 1995

A blood stone, sharpened
Enchained enriched,
A tear drop of history
Enfocusser of pathways.Theft?
Murder? Fraud? Maybe something
Stronger, more serious?
A blood stone symbol of clash
 And Liars and looted for money
(with lyre, lute and cymbal).
Fiersome dangerous ornamental
Always in the service of mankind
Worthless until crushed to fine dust
(Remains of cremated bones of history),
And used to make this Tissot swiss guard watch.

Blood Stones

Circa 1995 (subsequently amended)

Myriads light multiplied
The satellite remains of a planetary gem

Asteroidally yours but two a penny
Hot cross deep Blackwell blood read
Like Stones and Justice

Yours truly (madly deeply)
Now clearly, hear more fully
(That) somebody bought it
(Probably in exchange for drug paraphernalia)
Several thousand times over.

Strongly denying a verisimilitude
To reality, of course.
The blood stones bejewelled
In fifty three various shades of red
Glinting dangerously in the museum light.
Two human long bones, discarded in the muddy
Archaeology of anti diluvian Eocene Sheol
Nestle copiously, anonymously, broken in clay
Alongside the potter.
Could this blood red bloodstone
Have caused all this pre-historic anarche'?

Jigsaw Peace

c. 1995

At the washing stones of Standing Imperception
I remember... what?A ward round of important skills?
A timescale of privilege (now forever lost) A need?
That pointed camaraderie leading to grains of paranoia?
The pointed camaraderie leading to exile?
What, then? A burden of proof for a belief?
Noisy sleepless nights above the banging bar door?
Midnight calls to witness new life in deliverance?
Or blind panic in the filmy discovery of treachery and life
Real enough to cut and draw blood,
That twist as the blade of truth justifies its right to be in situ
(well, well, well, within its rights)...

Slowly the tethered donkey of Life, reluctant
To its Paschal mission drags its feet
Pulled to life by the great god Apollo
By chance our life obscures both death and dues
O'erpaid by Aesculapius in our name
Incompetent or not (open or shut)
This 'cervical case'
Is washed on the standing stones of im-perception
Forever and again...

Sisyphus and the Bloody Stones

January 2007

In ancient incantations Sisyphus' intones
Each day bound to push the rolling stones
Each day up, each night down,
Weary eyed with his candle-light and gown...

His neighbour 'bound Prometheus' having stolen Passion's fire
Considers 'S' something of a liar
When he complains of limbs and aching pains
That burn into the night, saying 'no pain, no gain'

By comparison Prometheus nightly lost his guts
As the squawking harpies drove him nuts
Ripping out whole yards steamed 'testine
(Which made it difficult for 'P' to drink his Ovaltine)

LOVE THY NEIGHBOUR AS THYSELF
Aint that the way uphill to heaven through to health ?

Extra! Extra! :

Heavy heavy water ban:
'Read all about it!'

Spring 2006

Burnt blood rhubarb red
Mixing not segregating
Flowing an instant in congealing milk bright white
Dealing violence destruction and the dead
Dead voice of hunger unbroken
Swollen bellied gorging monstrous
Mushroom cloud
Bloated as a post prandial dessert
Unrequired but obliging politeness
In those it serves its instrument
Choking humanity on the seeds of Eden's knowledge tree
Banishing by threat admonishing by threat
Writing its mis-shapen harvest on acid rain
A whole year's umbrella with which
To hold away the blindingly obvious problem of technologies' mad pursuit
Is this the way forward really?

Around the 20th anniversary of the Chernobyl tragedy

D' NAe Vince's Code

2006

When a muddle appears
That confirms innate fears
('Everybody else bar Me'
Invited to the All bar One pub).

Or nothing succeeds like success?
Sticky buns and digestive sympathy for tea?
Thank God for humour and Our Good Queen Bess

Is not quite how it might be.
Bending any light to be kind without fee
Is it in me to be happy?
To be free from things that are snappy
(You know crocodile sandwiches that are lunches
For somebody's spirit developing their hunches)
Quasimodo's such a draw he's almost a fashion (if it weren't for the bells)
'Quasi, don't get the hump please'
Notre Dame's finest carried his with him
Where'er he went...
But then you never quite know what to the tourist will sell...
Just being soulful pretty and slim ain't no sin
So take a view and plant a few
Close knit ideas that belong near a pew
And one day expect the flowers
To bloom from seeds that were planted under a bower...
Nostradamus foresaw not the medical
Role that Kraepelin, Bleuler and Korsakov imposed upon the wit,
Mulling on the nature of the indwelling catheter
Nor the WASP surgeon cutting the spirit
Of this self same foreigner student medic...

Now transforming from negative to positive
With only lack of faith in self
Blinkering my inner vision and health

Each broken strand of light, a broken voice
A broken wing a broken memory and maybe broken super-symmetry...
('Tiger tiger burning bright')
One of the remains of the day now, after (Beatles and) Beatitudes
And the feeding on the hillside by the Galilean
Five thousand at a time with a few grains of truth
(what is that between so many?)
And one of the twelve baskets full that was left over
For Tony Clare in the Community (European)
After studying the skill and the skull with all its 'genial tuberosities'

With no genuine genius gene locus to declare
How do I explain my fear of the Judas kiss?
And please Miss, can you help my receding hair?

Growing Up- Neurologic
(after Acker Bilk)

Staring up into Sicily's own *cote d'azur*
I feel a cerulean mantle remind me of an earlier world
Before I understood the meaning of bread unleavened,
Bittered herbs and lamb's wool thought.

Slow nuclearity in the sun ripened soil
Warms internally an ice cold beer
Melting this too,too solid non academic in the midday sun:
And though *I know (I think, therefore)*
-Slowly relaxing through this film
Of perception and misperception-
That I am merely sensing this euphoria
Due to the raised dopamine levels of my *nucleus accumbens*
And generally *my* brain's limbic system apparatus
I *can* share this common-sense with others
Who have known the same experience...

How do we dance to the music of time around these feelings?

What are the dance steps and politeness of etiquette and why
Am I now lonely as Auden's 'moping cormorant' or a seagull on the
        stranger's shore...occasionally.
But sharing in the joyous spirit of family and friends
Do I not thank God for charter flights and Holidays in the Sun
And Apollo in his Chariot and the healing of pain
        and the making of music and some fun...?

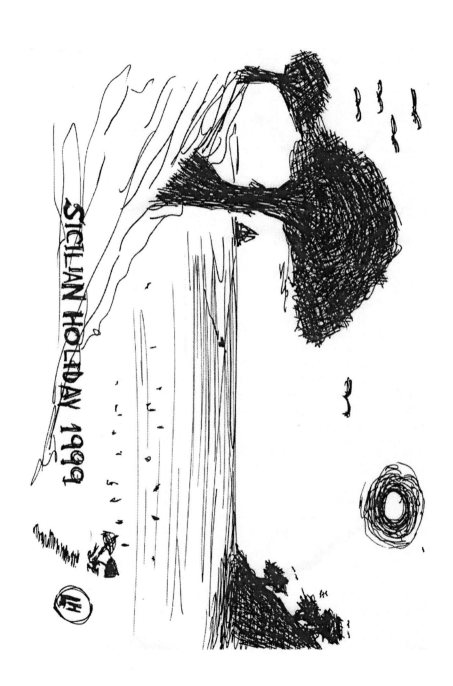

SICILIAN HOLIDAY 1999

63

Echoes of Addington, SA

(amended from original written 14/ 7/86)
Addington Hospital in the suburb of Durban, South Africa

How flimsy is this meld of life held tight
Only by a strand of love of self
How often do my moods alter with the weather
Only to align my attitudes with Ghibelline or Guelf
How graceless is this response that follows
On leeward from the very stuff
Houses are made of, from Sorrows'
 Real bricks, from friends' and partners'
Dropped-off-the-cuff
 Remarks Regarding Reputations and Relaxations...
Christ, that genius of Love and Life
Appears occasionally to resolve
All Problems (even Coronations,
Baptisms, Funerals, even Weddings),
Or other social milestone family event
Which Reflection intones and names
The Pascal Lamb its blood in shedding.
In Paschal Sacrifice by any Wife
Of Christ (Whyche nunne dare say), another Mother Theresa
To our rescue and our conflict came.
A Missionary Church's scent filled
Service a celebration might declare
In order that though we leave well, Clear-
Sobered From the Service 'In Memoriam'
 Yet we would feel blest and wiser
By the privilege of encounter
To Our own beautiful dear departed Mother,
Our own Sovereign Queen in Heaven.

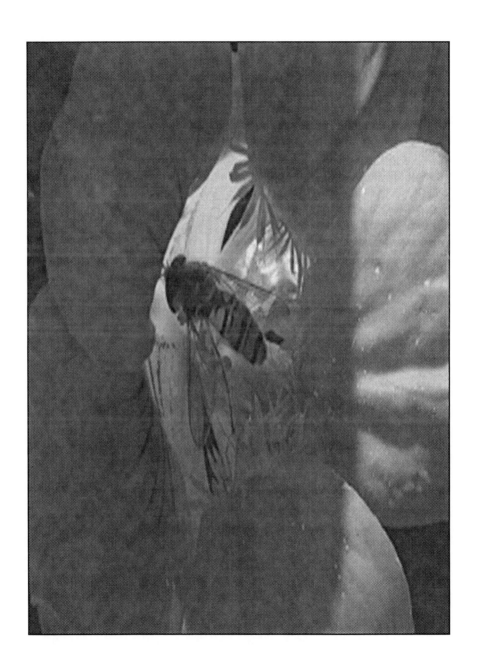

In Queue Gardens, W5

2006

Nunne so great
Nor yet nunne so wyse
As those who tell men there are no lies.
Neath each tempered tonsured pate
There lies a maelstrom inchoate
Of earthly Joy and Glorious Resurrection.
This Community, nay Soul Communion
Is a college clear and a ruling Benediction
Above the worldly anarche and menarche
Of this rough handled Word
(Especially of women kind).
It prizes them to place upon a pedestal
These Graces that they be looked on in condescension from above.
Nun so great (the innocent of Virginia Waters an aside)
As those who tell no lies nor never have or ever will have lied.
To the monk Women appear to be of virtues three
The Eve, mother to them all both blessed saint and martyred See
Second that Unsung heroine, a Virgin Mother, Mary Blessed be,
In azure as in gold that's true
As well the student bikes of Magdalene College heard
Acknowledged in the cold of old and third,
Studying of Humanity whilst praying for their true Oxford 'blue'
Be warned, the monk to each and every rose
Though smiling sweetness 'pon the nose
Along the stem its bloody thorn
By natural religion's rubrics' wiles exposed:
Defensive is this story borne...
As you or I of earthly pains are shorn
To walk barefoot upon these hallowed lawns...

Listening to My Body

LH
Written on Burns Night 2006
(remembering an incident in the operating theatre c1979)

Drawing down the blind of revelation
To each and every Host in distribution
(Every ending a beginning)
I imagine I sense the Placenta of Life
Tearing away from its root
And feel the sharpness of the Surgeon's Knife
As it skilfully separates me from myself, my mood
Which spirit heightened, sears across my ears like a scalded cat.
Not knowing I would be heard
And targeted to my waist deep river utterance: 'Merde!'.

Burning internally now, my 'spirit' slowly dissolving from within
I screamed into the silence of inner space (where no-one will hear)
Caught in the headlights of the here and the fear I welcomed my tears to begin
Voicing in sympathy the un-anaesthetised pain of the operated
As though I was that unborne child
(without the privilege of the condemned: the hearty breakfast)
Prematurely engineered into this world before my time (and worse) I
         co-operated
With the consultant's skill to send this student's pride
                  and faith reeling from first to last...
(thence went home to resume that hobby of intending
                  the quarts to fill the pintpots),
Reflecting feebly on 'the rights of man but not the unborne life-spots'...
Lurching from bear to beer to bier...
And then from there to hear.

From Here to God

10 August 1998
(amended slightly 1st Feb 2006)

Showing awesome restraint
The clergy man owing more to Barclays Bank
Than to RS Thomas and Iago Prytherch
Balanced on his Cycle
Of New Life for Old, young hopes for old pain
Turns his world view to view my world (and weep)
And though I witness no stigmata upon his palms
Did I not witness something
Like a tear shed slow and low?
And when having once rowed out
To meet this Fisher King
Upon his lakeside
Why did I not ask of him
"What ails thee, Father?"
" If only you knew the things that make for peace"
I heard him quote within my heart of hearts
As this Genesis twists the grain of truth his life sub-stands
Bearing his cross to Resurrection
Bearing tricolour fresh love (rubicund, white and green)
Expecting his hope and faith and love to save these stranger days,
Extending this answer to the questions posed by prayer
However long delayed by the story of the Flood
However bisected by the complex imaginaries of mathematical solutions
However dissected and put to rest as eternal knowledge (to keep our
          verities warm)
However often analysed and counter analysed by political persuasion
And cynically disregarded by pragmatic philosophical dissertation...

My parents and other family
Partake of this first of the Last Suppers
In a spirit of a time of future pasts
Mere rude mechanicals of prayer unopened until then
Who now turns to repair to supper to the sound of psalms
(After a luncheon fast for all his people, right there write then
 A true Job for Uz in our day and Christ man for us without comforter
          Eliphaz' qualms)

I am looked in the eye to witness in myself a change of heart and mood
Which to this day, still stands amidst all that might-be that is good,
Wherein before the pierced tragedy marked the slaughtered innocence,
The martyrs' memorials (of all shapes and sizes) was to me revealed
Which with due respect I must needs acknowledge
And remember as part of my new life in God...

A seed of hope and faith was planted (despite myself)
Most easily manured by the shivering of fear and isolation
Sprung up like the sign of Jonah the castor oil plant amidst the shadows
Casting shade for the three white tigers of Eliot's maginations
Three white tigers in Sicilian Leopard's skins
Aligned like the armorial bearings of Albion's past or future history
Even as European monasteries have always spoken in one tongue
Feeding on the remains of the day
(my liver, spleen and renal apparatus
 and this muscle known as flexor digitorum profundis)
This Roman, hungry as a turkey before its Christmas
Takes the simple twist of grain instantly changing it
Into Something out from Revelation
Unthinkingly grubbing up the morsel of Truth
And quoting WB Yeast to turn the 'something'
Into Spirit's breadth... both breath and bread.

Advice

Nottingham 13-12-06
A couple of days after a healing seminar in London

Avoid the moon (that rhymes with June)
Look up the calendar:
A Void: The howling moon
 Wanes as receding pasta water drains
                    From colander
Splashing onto the waxed and polished kitchen floor
Seek ye the sauce that opens up perception's door
The one true Genesis of us all
Avoiding the moon face
(Now pale and drained)
Of a Cushing patient's race
To save a life (heroic)
Cushioned and reflected in a script
Of sharpened teeth and bodies ripped
Produced and filmed in a chamber anechoic
'Seek ye high tide seek ye high noon'

O God this June before the Fall
Of Iridescent Gold Autumnal shades from off the Trees
While heavens' rays collide
                    Congealing leaves are stored in deep mid winter's freeze
While coughs and sneezes spread diseases
Every one looks out for spring's first call
Remembering last year's rejuvenated life wish
Between the worries of Ceres' winter spirit
And the wisdomed wit of renewed summer leases...

ADDICTION

13 -12-06
Again after driving overnight to Nottingham and for some reason
remembering taking blood samples from patients in casualty so long ago

Haemorrhaging into the Void
Need Appears: it has to be filled:
Distraction Release Analgesia:
What you will -No need to be annoyed
Just for the minute whatever it is frees you
To feed the need again: to empty out the void
Food itself to some is not so much a benediction as addiction
When the 'end of time' table is billed
And th'eternal waiter holds your earthly coat
And snickers as you say you've lost your ticket for the boat
Across the Styx: what was it that held such conviction?
Such inner sense such apparent clarity
That life itself was judged disparity?
That you focussed off from Life
And buried yourself into nothing
To feel the steely cut of the self inflicted steely needle knife
That you yourself (just for a flickering minute)
                    you thought was worth a something ...

Why me? Why here? Why now?
(Patient : orientated for person, place and time)

circa 1995(now amended)

At the party, old friends meet
New friends get to know each other
On their first day of their Physiology and Anatomy
'Russ this is Violet, Vi Russ'
As I observe, one more fly on the wall,
Impinging on our native outlooks. Viewpoints
Exchanged akin to spin as skin to skin encroaches
At the dance, kisses this side of the midnight pumpkin coaches...
Feeling terminally uncomfortable as I hear
The pressure wave in front of me deepen at the bow.
Ice cold in Alex I sail down south
Where I don't like this game of self deceit no more...
Carelessly breaking the ice with Lenin's ice pick at a party
'Imagine, Imogen , no Hello below us ,above us only spies'.
I feel the heat turned up as I start to 'Bjorn Again' away...
Except that now the servant leads the master
Pupils teaching gold to the good but ailing bus conductor
The tug will once more pull the ocean-faring
One liner out of Glower Star docs, a musicians' conductor.
Watching the Princess conduct her
Self through all and any minefields a hundred sundry times.
Heron smuggling (and all its empty promises and works)
        is a crime that no more washes clean
In the moneyed laundry-mart of Life
Than you could in a crystal shower...
Cohabiting in a little flat nestling each
                within our own power
That the docu-soap be walled in with Maximilian Kolbe,
Like eating people, it is wrong...
A scandal that gnawed at the ignored
Huskies in the freezing waste
 seeking out the north by north west passage...
Meanwhile in a frozen outhouse in LA
The terminally ill Xerxes sips on chicken broth all day
As the burning broth dribbles out his chin
Young Orestes tends his old protagonist without sin
And bids him fond farewell in knowledge of the End
And prays to some or other higher God to make amends.
Like ancient Romans Keats and Shelley when they said their last...

Stand and Deliver

Autumn 2005

Do I remember the acid burn of cordite in my nostrils?
Do I remember the recoil of horror
When the rifle butt first punched my shoulder?
Do I remember breech loading...?

When I attended that breech loaded birth
The registrar, sweating at midnight in the closed shop theatre;
Finally the baby boy delivered by forceps
'May the forceps be with you'
Uttered his crystal clear cry unto the world...

As I screamed into the night A fortnight later from a dream
Like Arthur Janov under a bridge in a scene from that film
Cabaret...

Did I then remember the sarn't major shoutin'
At me to keep the standard issue Lee Enfield high above my head
At the risk of doing un-nameable things to my ability to procreate?
Above my head as though surrendering to Fate
And public school ethos and cadet corps rations
Wandering through water or whatever...
Remembering that *lex non curat de minimis*
The law does not concern itself with *trifles*
But rather shows preferment for main course fish and chips
And the process of the peace
Not just the desserts of vast eternity at all...

Does that remind me of the smell of something rotten in my nostrils?
Something in this State of Denmark still?

Walking with the Divine

14 -3-06

The spring Magnolia not yet burst
Into its flowering bloom
And from the earth not yet drinking in its thirst
Green dormant life in tantric divine expectation
Clearly is enraptured within an earthy cogitation
 Of warmer holier days of still remembered summer
O'erhead a woodland creature builds
                its rhythmic beat as Nature's drummer
While Beauty walks along her Sylvan path
The squirrel and the crow and duck all laugh
At human frailty, for desired Nature's beauty
To steward ancient prehistoric time today, again is bounden duty
So that we may hear the spirit of th'eternal
             coming through belittled lives
And strengthen our humanity with what has always been:
To hear again the vegetating reborne life unseen
Is to know that summer comes sincerely as rebirth

To hear the sounds of nature through
          The noise and haste of science
Is to meditate upon our life, our worth, in clearest conscience
To hear and realise the depth and breadth of spirit
Is to walk with kindness and Humility in Grace
Is to hear the squirrel's crying for its mate and honour it
In this spirit of sympathy and compassion most profound
And as Spirit taught us we must obey
And thank the Lord of all Creation as we pray...

Spring in Richmond Park

14-3-06

Overcast is the morning
 The afternoon bids a cheerful warning
Of brighter weather and some concerns.
Intent on listening to the quiet of the open
I hear the counterpoint to silence :
          the gliding aery sounds of woodwind
Rising through despondent cloudy feeling
                    like the wing'd bird soaring high
Aloft on thermal draughts that rise
Like Lazarus from out the cave
Commanded by the Naturality of God-made-man
To open up my eyes
I come out walking
Into the light and newness of my life
To reappear from out the gloomy dank
And shed these bandaged ribbons
          of tethered bound mortality that stank
Like bounden flesh risen from the cave and saved
A buffet from the wind awakes me from this reverie
In interpretation of these forces elemental-
I await a friendship with this Nature
(one more aspect of God's Tri-une Gift of Life to us)

And listen to my fearful fret of words
Cascade from out my mind amidst the buffeting of the wind...

In Good Faith?

February 2006

The palimpsest of time wiped clean
And another tablet of perception is re-writ
In a cycle of rebirth...
Since nothing is written in tablets of stone
 (as the wise ones say)
'Cept perhaps the priestly mantra
'Remember man that though art dust
and unto dust thou shalt return'

...My beginning is my end...
(And is my end in life to begin again anew?)
For in the end the love you take is equal to the love that you create
And the karma and beginning of tomorrow's world;
Inner earth gives birth to life
Through artesian pressure well of Alice Springs
 Hope eternal giving rise to floodlight,
                              inner insight and white light.
While amidst the February squalls and blue skies
The palimpsest of life wipes clean
And the stylus writes more waxen works
(and having writ moves on?)
As another tablet of perception is re-writ...

' We Still Need a Miracle Mr Jones '

1997?

Watching 'doctors-to-be' on tv
Drowsily I reflect on my muse:
Dwelling on some 'four last things'
 (heaven, hell, death and judgement)
And th'accelerated developments of some would be medic-clergy
Ever holier, ever younger policemen in the news
Ever more devoted even beyond their preaching tones;
All year saints (not just plastered for this Advent or that Lent)
Practised to ever deeper feats of prayerfulness;
So 'other worldly' that parallel quantum wormholes need be booked
Well in advance In order that your appointment with them
                                    not be wasted nor overlooked
So accurate and precise in their stitching
                         seemingly beyond even clinical audit
By all accounts that their merest whispered intonations
                      Are able to move mountains of morbidity
Their very essence a proclamation of their own 'quiddity'
That sense that *'super materiam ignis triumphans'*:
Their passion should melt the ice
Of *'Lex non curat de minimis'*
Which is really N.I.C.E.
As it settles on their greying hairlines
Deconstructing first Love then Life
(amidst the 'bons mots', 'petits verres' and fine wines)
Leaving behind them,the 'hoi polloi' in confusion and stupidity...?

Ice and fire, fire then Ice, bit and byte wisdom and insight
As they observe their own alexithymic denial of Lifespans
Touching ever more gently with their probing fingers
                                    Life beyond the Kiss
Hand in glove excelling at this work they love
Beyond the coiling writhing Aesculapian DNA snakes and Freud
Their 'religion' requires them not to linger for another pint
                                    In 'The Son and Dove'...

Has academic freedom really come to this ? Heaven's Above!
Equally well versed in aspects of 'paralysis agitans' as 'movements, athetoid'
These would be saints confide in all humility only in Themselves
And signal to their staff to deal with patients with patience...
I remember some benignly enlarged urine flask
And the nurses hushed and reverential whispered
                              exhortations(in good conscience)
For me to endure again the Sacrament of 'The Passing of the Water'
As though through arid deserts of bones bleached white midst the
                midday stones
My piss might flow into a stream and then a river
'We still need a miracle Mr Jones'
Rather like some expert might refer to a 'spleen' or some or other 'liver'
Said as though in the middle of a Christian Church
In hushed and reverential tones but just loud enough for
                              everyone to hear and snigger ...
Just as an English Cricketer might whisper on the Test's
Last day at Lord's to th'eternal umpire, his own Life giver
As though beating India at a game of cricket was somehow worthy
Of Bernadette of Lourdes
('Like the Madonna Virgin' but without the funeral pyre
Or the Transvaal necklaced burning rubber tyre)

Instead
It is for me the start of all my fears
As the would be surgeons draw their swords
And write their points pon my belly
While wishing that I hadn't watched that telly...

I look for St John's Wort but find only St John's Wood not Lourdes
(But who needs aspirin spin when WG Grace can help you win)
Reeling blindly 'bout these midday stones and bones
I mutter 'sotto voce' to my self (and others)
'We still need a miracle Mr Jones...'

Time

At the eleventh hour at the eleventh minute

On the eleventh month the Guns stopped.

And because Nature abhors a vacuum

The first jagged shoots of poppy leaf

Pushed up out of

the Dead

Earth..

PEOPLE

A Foggy Day in London Town

2003

When I cannot because I do not
Dare to argue with reality
When I cannot see because my mood
Is darker than ebony and as real as wood, I should
Close my eyes and think on practicality
But I do not because I cannot

Instead I look for the Light of some words;
But words carry meaning when they are heard
Words can wield power as heavy as the clashing of swords
Words can light potions and brew up some witchery
(Words might evoke the spirits of treason and treachery)
Words can bear feelings - words flashed onto ceilings
Like numbers portending some sort of dealings
Scratched on a wall: each one a meaning but not for us all
Words are like keys that open us up
And join us to spirit as we sit down and sup.
 And there are words that like beacons
                         (Of bad yokes of egg-heads)
 That Shine out like lighthouses all through our gloom
When the words that appear in our dreams when a'bed
Are the words that Ms Woolf in the bloom of her youth thought
                    Brought only doom
Can with a twist of a phrase and strong deep sunrays
Thin out the fog with a bright radiant smile
Like the 'beacons and eggs' of fresh hatched ideas
As we crack a new joke as we drink on our beers...

Communion, Too

2002

Stormy as petrels follow the trawl
(The sun setting low, now getting small)
Dipping, diving, gliding on air
Nets full of fish too much to bear,
Walking on wind, fighting for scraps,
Faith undivided, still, there at its source.
Foul mouth'd fishermen, good men and True
Sharing their Mind, strong without lapse,
Discover the captain, my captain, who might give the clue
How to steer through the thunder, lightning and rain,
Back to the port, their record unstained.
To their families home now,
Their labours rewarded, beer –wiping brow,
These are the seamen that is the life
Stormy as petrels who follow fisher and knife,
The yellow sou'westers glisten with oil
As visible reminder of the whole of their toil
The familied ship gives way to families real
As the sacrament marriage invokes all its seal.

Moon waxes lyrical in the cusp of a glass
The froth cleared away, good will steals within,
Sharing communion (and all without spin)
Discourses the rules of how to live free
To believe without Pride, it's deepest of joy
To live and to love and all without sin
To sail into windward, and to pitch at its lee,
Where stormy crowned petrel dives into sea,
Is to be at the cross to acknowledge its Loss
Is to remember the story of how he was borne
To live in the Temple whose Curtain was Torn

Remember, remember the 'hammer and nails'
Where humanity's end became its reprise,
(Humanity saved becomes humanity bailed),
Humanity clever sometimes forgets the divine
Except where possession becomes all that is Mine...

To seek out the higher between God and the buyer
Is Miraculous, real, to remember to pray
To the Purchaser Royal of all of our souls
And Praying for Peace is what we must needs say
For words without feeling maybe heaped upon shoals...
Both Christian and Fisher
Freeman or Slave
We gather our catches
And speak in dispatches
Of all that well wisher
Was able to save
For everyone now and everyone then
For all that we know and all that we ken
Is magic indeed, injustice repealed
It makes families happy
Strong friendships are sealed
While explorers provided trustworthy maps

We pray to our God
Like petrels on sea
And hope for those scraps
That will make us feel free...

Reflection

The sound of local bells in the mist echoes through the years
In a smell of damp and expectation
Sandstone to sandstone
   intelligence in churches reaching out for sub-Stance
To the Sky Cloud Ahead. There is no turning back
Black yellow pale white face self examination
In good faith and conscience and common sense
To experience some pain now
So as not to leave unremembered
Greater torments of Works unfinished
And charities unchequed.
Taxing this man's goods and that man's talents
There is no hope of cure
Or jammed up like a freshly devoured
Sandwich of reality
The winds of change blow away
More missed opportunities in Time
And Judgement absolute (though not absolute)

Praise the Lord

With Liar, Loot and Symbol...

Practical Hints for Prospective Horsemen of the Apocalypse
(with a foreword on theories of Death, Sulphur and Plague)

1997/1998

Before setting out on a long journey
Check your steed, he may be too sanguine
Drain off some blood, like veal, until he stands pale with greed.
Make sure you have located correctly targets for devastation
Nothing annoys God more than procuring
       Revelation upon the wrong   population...
If you see children crying chuck in a few *Drosophila melanogaster*

After all the media loves nothing more than marasmic
 children too frail
          to swat their own flies...

If deciding to burn down town and gown with sulphur
Ensure that you use International Standard Yellow Sulphur
Often horsemen in the past have mistakenly used the wrong sort of sulphur

Whole areas have been covered with the fine dust
Which though initially thought sound volcanic ash
Was nothing other than the topsoil of Chernobyl
finally settling from out the clouds...

Finally when visiting morbidity upon all God's planet
Of the hungry and poor and leprous
Always ensure they are the last to realise that
 their medical insurance won't cover "Acts of God"
Though what benign entity would act like that is yet to be discovered

Poetic Licence Applied For...
(No. 5UE 02159)

Spring /Summer 2006

After the funeral service in Rome
Flying high above *le montagne*
Snow capped cloud capped tow'rs
Wrapped in a bubblewrap of gas with wings,
 Is to lean back and trust in God,
 Is to *hear technology through the air*
 To set the circle square:
To hear the harmony and music of the spheres in 'things being various'
Is as finding 'le mot juste' in the books and papers scoured;
To let logic and emotion chat is not so odd...
Nor to take solace from the half-bottle 'Vina Albani'
On your in-flight table
Chatting with your family
Is but to reconcile that which is,
With that that might have been...
From the first of Bethlam's stable

Three Mixed Messages (Jerusalem plc)

LH
Written 2007 using fragments originally penned 1980

None so deaf as those who will not hear
No greater distance than between two points
If the intention is thus:
(but then there is no greater love
Than to lay down one's own life... the Good Book says)

The *mind at its ebb reveals the stones of which it is composed*
Sometimes I used be

The *agnostic who believes in God*
The sun worshipper expecting soft rain
Everyman on a Pilgrim's Progress
And the diary of a nobody, still...

And Now?

Now I pray that I believe
That by my fruits I will be known

Now and then over the years....

The Interpretation of Dreams

12-3-06

Like the graceful gliding swan
In a revelation of the church of Laodicea
Our own 'Queen' Lady Seer appears serene Within,
(Without th'unseen turmoil of her soul
Belied by the fretful agitated left side digitations
  Digging-in the worry-of the dirt of pain
  Of all the places in Humanity's deep hurts),
Has again her mastery o'er Paine appeared
As Nature in the flow of harmony in Words
  Despite those glaring telltale 'hidden' signs...?

Her voice relax 'd
                as the flowing waters of repose
Is redolent of a riverbank
                lined with flowering rose.
The swan's harmony ill befits
                that inner turmoil
(And is ill served)
                by glaring light
Of Wisdom-clear her display of insight bright...
Reducing humanity to a source
Will oft blind the innocent (of course)
                with her ferocious brand new caritas
Her majesty and dignity will surpass
Into the unconditional love of God (at Source)
For all of us in our Felled Humanity
                and loving kind
For her fellow man
                and families' loving values:
Thus her Crowning Restoration's Comedy
                and familiar family's Familial Glory...
Whether it Be
        Social Justice and its Great,
                Good Intent for shared humanity,
Or merely re-enactment
                through some faith and works...

92

To the deeper mystery Of God's love for us
                                    we follow...
To the point of understanding and beyond ...

Now thank we all our God
Our source of all and all that's Good...
That Spirit has affected as it should

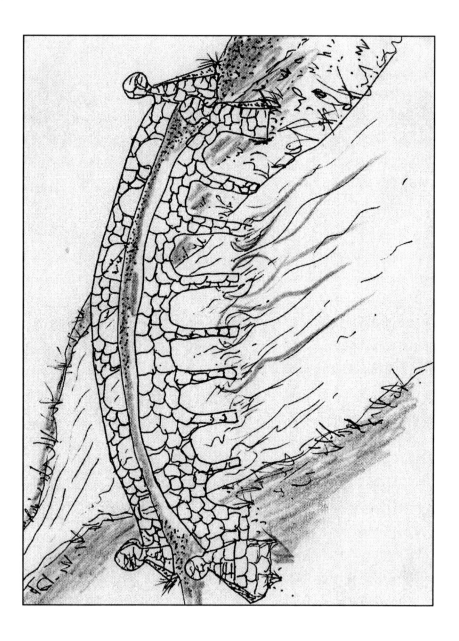

A Quiet Afternoon by the River?

18 Feb 2006

At the dull day of the river crossing
Where the energy is low and the water flat
Broken reflection of some building works
Darkening the reflected grey light sky
Looking for peace I settle to write
First one group huddles to a stop
Talk and walk on by then back
As I have done myself
When someone dares to paint outside...

A smoker's hacking cough breaks through the silence
Which effect disturbs the geese
To fly off in all directions to squawk and honk
As a small air filled lifeboat judders into life
Moving affront its tiny V-shaped wake
Conflicting (but to no avail) across
The heavy wash a passing tourist boat creates
At the bridge the trundling train's underground musical rhythms
Ensures inclusion in this scenario
Disturbing the gulls into a panic of random oscillation
About some unknown source
Signalling an urban perturbation in their midst
Another train comes in across the river into Town
Across the bridge as the jogger softly pads his path along the way...

This tired afternoon by the river
My only thought is of stuffing cotton in my ears...

4 oclock Saturday Afternoon
Kew Bridge Walk way

February 2006

By rivers edge I watch the boat
Playing in the spray. The aircraft flying
Over Kew's Botanicals interrupts the rolling gloom
As passers by walk on, I notice nothing
And nothing noticed me
I think on heaven's four last things
(Which somehow in the gloom
befits the winter quietude)
And pray for rhythm's roots' new life
To re-emerge when Ceres from her Hades is released
I want to reach up and push through to light
As I feel the need to stretch from out this ground.

On the Riverside

Listening out amidst the conversation for 'les mots justes'
All I hear is the murmuring of the city at rest
A grey sky and a break of laughter –a spirit of relaxation
Which though unplanned may not be thus unwarranted
I worry that I waste my self holding onto something
That like a heaven sensed far exceeds my grasp
Like reality to this fool
I look to wisdom but wisdom is not there
As if Mother Nature is tired and needs a holiday
And cleverness has hung its coat up
St Clements in my hand I sip on ice

Asking whether the little life that onto daddy holds
Pointing out the builder's crane across the shore
("Cra! Cra!" I hear that wee bairn cry)
Will realise the truth but know not more
Than anyone who stands to watch the squawking geese
Coming into Land from whence they came,
And write to tell their story of a walk along the Thames...

Kew Bridge
Saturday Afternoon

18 Feb 2006

The love-lorn orange crushed walks by along the water's edge
As doctors share concerns about budgets in a hospital in Fleet
A television news reporter's 'sound bite' as he walks on by:
'Nothing much will come of it'

A family of four all recite their daughter's poem:
"...Twelve little girls in two long lines..."
Followed by a whoop of laughter and content...

I hear the screeching gulls as the geese squawk their own dissent
A restaurant spills out the door as four walkers discuss their Labradors
And as I head towards the bridge at Kew
I hear a human cry from out some boats
I look but do not see a soul
And cannot see the ripple in the tide
where once a person rowed...

At the Waters Edge

29/6/06

Outside the Bull's Head, by the bridge at Barnes
Parochially watching both the 'fours' and sculls
Pulling oars in time behind their mentor's speedboat
 In its wake... I watch and thinking pleasant
                    thoughts in the orange setting sun,its charms
 Apparent, observing of both the solitary sea's gull, way inland
And the full spanned dark clad crow as it dulls
The pavement 'neath its flight and height
Thinking on my brother's splinter but not mine own mote
Holding on to thought with pen in hand
Scratching out a life in pen and ink like a life in river's sand
Appearing as a land worm seeking for something lost in sight
Aware that now as always affirming what I say I do, I can,
I ask of God, this wretched Caliban and pagan, asks of God
'What I should do?' (now ain't that odd?)
'Which is the way forward through the Human Zoo?'

Do I not ask for riches? Know . Neither Licence
To observe God's wonder to meditate in silence
God's gift of wisdom and right choice...
I do not fly above the crowd in strong full voice
To raise me for a Magick moment within the midst of angels
Up above this earth-bound tongue-tied misfit seeking Tintagel's
Mystic treasured shore, looking for an earthen cache in which to hide
Within the lapping radio labelled Thames-side lungwort tide...

Looking out over the edge
At lowish tide, seeing bubbles in the sand
And a billowing plastic bag wedge
Itself just out of reach of hook or hand...

I count the feeding ducks head down within the silt
Quack quack one two three four five

That setting orange sun atop the flaming tree tops
 Which stops the day as it began...

'As above then so below'
'... come in cielo cosi in terra...'

And as I hear the others' glimpsing heaven
 I count two more ducks, six, seven
Quack, quack, quack...quack QUACK !

 I hear the brown and silted holy water Thames
Like Ganges' distant healing shores crack
Wide this early morn's tired, long- forgotten aims
While I by the tide of Humber wouldst complain
Of Agues and chills and fevers (few), and pains,
 Miasmas and the rigors (red setters in the setting son,)
All pointers to the cognoscenti of the way ahead
While lusty oars men in the water dip their blades for fun
Humanity to salvation, by joy in Nature, is potentially ably led...and One

S P Q R(Sono Pazzi Quelli Romani)

Chelsea Physic's Gardening Tip

What is a quark?

Queried the friends of 'Muster Mark'

While hunting for the snark

Why 'tis just the sound of the posh duck's bark!

Came back th'espied remark!

A nonny mouse(age 49 and 3/4)
writing in his house partaking of the waters...

Cross and Blackwell

May/June 2006

Pater noster qui est in caelis...
This morning I stumbled down the altar steps
Following that Good Fellow, Horace, with his *'tardive dystonia'*
An ordinary fellow doing extraordinary work despite a Parkinsonian curse...

Last week my fellow helper dropped a handful of hosts to the floor
No doubt praying to his unsung heroine, Our Lady, his malady un-nursed.

This week as I stand at that same altar of self sacrifice
                              (within an altered state of mind)
I feel the holy shenanigans about me like a sacred wind
Swirling around my doubts and fears: my inner convictions lost , unheard
Though I have been here before, a thousand years it seems,
Saying softly spoken magic words
Around an *obligation* to profess my faith in Corpus Christi College
Holding onto dreams of physiology and Medicine within this world
And the sanguine spirit contained within
A chalice full of broken pieces that is, that is Light, which you may see,
But what so often feels like a whole host of broken promise
                    and mis-
                        broken wings (which you don't, as maybe,)

Pointing to a deeper world than this
                              a higher love
With something of a blind sight which now I no more hear....

So I say something: 'Ave Maria'
    and pray that I believe...)

In Memory Of Philip Lawrence

Originally Jan 1996
Philip Lawrence taught and inspired a lot of people at school (myself
included). He was also a member of our parish.

Against the blue remembered mountains
Along the Apennine Way, north of Rome
Where, *'If it be Human,*
'I hold nothing alien' to paraphrase Terence
Against the backdrop of those cloud-capped towers
Encrypted in a thousand years of mortgages and mortgagees,
Condominia and political dispute,
Standing alone
       To answer for the missed opportunities of this life
I simply present (strong silent memories)
Which elicit early purgatories even at 10 to 6 (or 5 to 5).

In the morning of the day or off to the evening show
Without a thought for those blue remembered mountains,
The market opens against the backdrop of a railway station
Built for the *'Coppia Mondiale'* now closed forever and just a coffee shop.
Gathering dust In May, Jejeune in June
Not very august through August
And no coolin' out the embers of November...
This is our lot if all we are is flesh and bone.

Remembering Romans, Friends and Countrymen
 And those blue remembered hills
In all their native glory
Quite literally remain unnoticed
But always present
Like the Apollonian Sun Above the clouds
In their influence
On History and geography
And philosophy of difference.

So why should the good man
Be victimised as he stands his ground
A good man's heart is hard to find
But a cheap and tawdry knife is not
In the cycle chain clash of today's lost light .

May he look on to remember
Us from high above those pagan mountains
In the spirit of the risen Christ
And forgive us our iniquities
Within our own hearts and works.

VALEDICTIONS
A triad of quarks

~

Thoughts on the death of a Friend

In Memoriam Paul Mellor 14/03/01

Paul's life crossed this path as though by chance.
Pompe's maybe, a shell like arrogance
Spun its orbital electron charms
Around himself like the Lord at the dance
Even as the torrent raged and the sea becalms
He knew he had the faith to walk on up
The gift of confidence was his bequest
Something that all of us, old or pup
Would qualify and put to test

When crossed he was as difficult as a problem
And his opinions he would let us know
His views should they be shared or aired
Were without omission always 'right'

So now he leaves us feeling low
(as he himself was, once his mania left him)
And though in his life he lived unpaired
And his father told us of this last and ultimatum
None of us in this journey into light will be spared
But one so young and vibrant with intelligence
Whose life's obituary will not be written for tawdry pence
Has visited us this last ten years
And graced us with humanity good and bad
And now he leaves us feeling mad and sad
To charm his heaven's gate as he charmed his life
(Don't the Gods of Greece love the ones that do their dying young?)
He will be there in his ascendant
Talking to his mentor(even with his tutor)
Discussing problems and putting the worlds to rights no doubt
But should his spirit in the cold of night shiver across aspects
of our physic(And not accountants bung)
This history of English and geography of the world
His charms and strangeness up or down
Top, bottom, truth, beauty
Are just the knowledge of his homage
To his Lord and master Christ
Through friends and family
Who grieve still for good *Paul Mellor*
In Ealing as in their Devonian homes and houses.

Robert McBain, Neighbour and Actor-an impression in Eulogy

Gentleman Bob, man of many parts,
Opened our eyes and our minds and our hearts
To that which is Truth
That which is light that which is free...

A man for all seasons and a man full of reason:
A man full of passion who just LOVES cake and tea.
Yet able of tragedy (with deepest humanity)
To draw in concupiscence
Then feed out cathartic those feelings so deep
That cling to our tears and well up our fears...
Tears that flow free, fears that sincerely
Like crops burnt out black
Are yet able to resource and emotions sustain
Are the spirit of love we follow and know:
That was the Man that was that Life.
He was that actor he had that Knack;
We look to ourselves and feel that his loss
Has made us aware that God lets us feel Pain...

The man who had painted, with a line his image defined
A man with that gesture the actor refined
Was the man of intelligence and knowledge Soviet,
Was the man who would garden
And listen with care, not regret
A man who liked walking to take in the air
A man whose box brownie dared capture the moment
Shared with us feelings his images, moods...
A man who would teach us if learning we should
Was the man who loved life and whose life loved him back...

Semi-Breve, Crotchet, Quaver :
(Bilbao Haus Blues three-four time)

Bill Parslow (who helped this young family move into their house becoming a friend to us) IN MEMORIAM 03/06/01

Billy the jazz, builder, of the syncopated rhythms
Comes to our door in the middle of a schism,
Between me and mine hears the heartache and the unvoiced anger,
Without foundation and discusses the prospect of building houses
       closer and stronger.
Drawing up well from those innate internal resources ,
He adopts adapts and discourses
On kitchens and jazz, damp-courses
And art, literature and conservatories,
While still useful with the old blockage in the lavatories.
Over time his jobs were to repair and rebuild
Construct and unblock, his reputation skilled:
He now no longer needs fear climbing the slates
(Clearly not averse to a night on the tiles)
Even as now he can see for miles and miles and miles ...

Hear how his notes hang in the air with angelswings
Between the nature of things and the GREATS

One Hundred (not out)

circa1995

As the bloodstone
Beckons
(always reminding me that
The Biblical Tower of a
hundred foreskins
Must have
Taken a lot of building)
I stop pull back and walk on up...

I notice a smudge of red where
Percy Bysse Kissed Mary Shelley
And rubbed her belly (full of jelly)
And then the glint of red
As heart crossed stones wave back
Across the bank of Charon's mooring
And blood red stones have crossed the Styx
And blood red rivers of life run
Around the Island of the 'unmentionable event'
In blood red sands reflected in one life
Under a red Missouri sky...

In some or other theatre.

The Other Patient

1998

Like a patient etherised upon a table
The anaesthetist lights another cigarette
The surgeon's blades seem stable:
But the banker's ward is now in debt
So now no more discussion
The hospitals are closing: Hey! But after lunch percussion!

Theory of music not cerebral concussion?

And now a contract has been signed
(Mephistopheles is not my name)
And gynaecologists, holy, fined
Today we shrink the NHS
And Napoleons all (but one)
We intrinsically appreciate
Our lives are in accountants' hands...

Praise the Lord

With Lyre, Lute and Cymbal...

CAT PEOPLE

Words Worthy of Life?

14-11-06

Annie, to her black and white cat
Humphrey (and all his jazz)
Wearing his fine DocSeuss hat
Quoth, "Life can be a Gas"...
And in kindnesse white is well gowned
Long used to listening without frowns
Gazing through experienced years
Delving through this forest of fears
Lights a spark and magnifies the Sunlight
That consumes like fire through Crystal bright
Drawing down th'eternal verities
Chisels the strong soul into a shape
Becomes the material of the mason's skills
Manipulates and edits with this life
Into a Something-worthy of all Eternity
Joining heart to heart within the Greatest's Cape
Seamless as the need to balance finance for the bills
Always appearing always to participate without strife
Without dispensing of the values noble such as Justice
Fulfilling Law by Laws of Love into a godly practice.

Humphrey the Cat!
(basking in the light of Life)

If you look at a mirror
And the sun is checked by its reflection
So that light and laughter come a little nearer
And memory coincides with natural thought selection
A smile within, your victuals soon untense
Forgetting that cold wind of rejection to the senses...
Open the windows and say hello to sunshine
Streaming through your opened eyes like the wine
Of celebrations and rejoicing in the good times past.
Where is the brand new day? Hold fast
To your belief, for are we not all outclassed
By God's Love (in his Promethean Winged Chariot)?
Be you Life's wretched homeless rebel
Or laughter's sanguine patriot
Does not dawn's early sunshine well
And gently melt the stubborn icy pain of life away
From each and every brand new day?

Humphrey the Cat, too

In and out the parlour up the Sherrye Tree
Geo-mantric insight focussed onto birth
Curving space-time compress displacing something free:
 How this spirit, of its gravity, is now a thing of worth not mirth ...

Humphrey in his jazzed up collar avoids the pilgrim's cuff
Padding cross the paving stones up onto a wall
Surveys the scene before him and glories in his stuff
Licking clean his silken fur and arches to stand tall...

Granite faced inscrutable he pads across the rooms
Scratches at the bed post pushes past the door
He sees his skein of wool but to his milk he zooms
Were it not for Mother's kindnesse he really would be poore...

Now curling up into a ball he snuggles by the fire
Though all outside is icy he really is quite warm
(Don't cross his path as mouse though, this really would be dire)
To snuggle up to sleep all day now *is that not surely true to form* ...?

Sybil

14-11-06

Always the diviner of spirit
The Sybil makes her choice and intuits
That which is now from that which is when
Harmonied rhapsodied, melodied Zen
Appears out of chaos like a firebird phoenix
Since life's little problems you can't always fix
Follow her days for good are her ways.
Compassionate soule who gives All her whole
One hundred percent Spirit's intent:
Reminds us our life from God it is Lent

Humphrey the Cat(4)

November 2006

Tiger, tiger burning bright
      Alwaies ready to the light
Separate out the good from evil
'Ready Strong and Able':
As go-between twixt earth and spirit
Helping kindly Man intuit:
The Sacred Lamb's Conduit To all of us from beyond the Fall
 From Earth's Orizon in a spirit of Jung's reborn and Rising Sun..
 Thus the cropped circle now is squared:
God is Love and Love is all (so God is all?)

And of Love's equal is there none?
(But the money's in the bank this month)
 Since Ever God's good Moshe crossed the burning sands
              Whence came he from Egypt to a distant Red Sea Land
Protected by the working of the Sacred Source within
 (and up Above Our topmost thoughts)
 And Long before the Holy Family's confinement in the stable
And long before the star shone down 'pon Angels' Quire
                  round yonder *Gesu' Babe*, well
Wrapped in swaddling clothes of Light and Love and Life...

Shamans and Sybils had attuned to Spirit White:
Upright, wholesome studious bright
 Along the Eastern camel path
Came Caspar Melchior and Belthashazar...

Soon we'll hear an interpretation and own views write
Reflecting crystal lenses treasured focussed Light;
Life coached Wisdom through those tricky paths
That Lead to life and Good and Promised Lands of Peace...

Pray speak in Confidence, Relax, and be at One with Self,
      But be ready and guide a ready laugh
Discover the way, 'Cat-Like' find your own way home
And Of the world and understanding to your self declare...

Relieve the ague in you yourself (without a doubt)
        and remedy the chill and fevers
                (and thereby cure all your own diseases?)
Be independent like 'the Humphrey about'
                        (so when you fall you'll land upright).
And of losing Faith in the Divine? Beware!
                        That fish they just won't bear to bite.
As you wait to see th'esteemed physician
Don't be phased when asked 'witch doctor do you want to see?'
(though most folks just want to see the television)
'Cos sometimes that is how it has to be ...

'Through a Glass Onion Darkly'
(a piece that passes understanding)

November 2006

Bending the light of thought through a nexus of material science
Geo-sophy of experience, philosophy of conscience
Climbing the Rushmore Rock face, Humphrey the Cat,
In a scene from that film 'Vertigo' (or North by North West?)
The feline Cary Grant (in a hat from Dr Seuss,
                              frock coat and tails, doing what he does best)
Perceives intones and smells the way through that
Maze of fear that brings both boy and girl to Mother Nature's hem...

Crystal packing MoMI separates yolk from white, good joke from bad,
Subject from the thing itself, allantoin sac from albumen
And all of *us* from all of *them*...
Christianity from Dark matter, Jerusalem from Islamabad
KwaZulu Nation Justice from Tutu's darkest energy
Immunological anergy from anaphylactic shock
Truth from Reconciliation
From despair and anarche a nation
A sense of direction from a Rock
Or anything else you care to roll up to want to hear
From here to there without despair ...
Set sail full square.

COLLARED AND CUFFED

~

The Lament of Nicholas Breakspear
(what ails thee father?)

circa 1997

Beyond the olive groves of buildings
that click the
presence of peace-keeping
technologies within

Beyond the orange efficiency of Sicilian
                                hill farmers
Beyond the orange rainbow warriors
                Of in laws
Beyond the bitter memory of
                        Greenjackets (and other outlaws)
Beyond the twisted confusion
                of obsessive stone throwing
                        identities
Beyond the horror of the definition of war
                Bodies piled high remote
                Even unto death
        and dying
Beyond even belief, immediate philosophy
 And clamouring reconciliation
Of the stock exchange at the end of day

Beyond the market of the here and now
Which as always spells nowhere, man (at times end)
Beyond the understanding of mere words or the squarerootofminusone
Wielded like the mantra of emotional armour
Shielding (in the mantrap) from
The onrush of too many discharging neural *boutons*
Surfacing as mania, epilepsy or distinctly odd strange ideas
'I only want one thing: another year at medschool' I add *post facto*
Or other paraphrase of desensitising grief
(which means five or six such
Theological errors all at once)

When as simply as a clinical sign was elicited skilfully, merely the
The consciously hypnotised evocation of presence of mind
Located by definition in the worst day of your life...
(which by now means the multiplication of problems by all accounts)...
Beyond the quiet despair of eyes around the grave
Speechless beyond the bark of a dog
Opening another door into the dark, dank earth
Even as it is forever firmly locked behind them now
(until the next world appeared unto Heaven)
And at the hour of our own demise
Beyond the drop jawed insensitivity of pugilist and publican alike
Beyond this writing on the wall
Moves Daniel's *'Mene mene takil parsin'*
Of having to listen write observe
That deeply corrodes the existence of ironic filed poetics
Of Primo Levi and his *'If Not Now When'*
Beyond the presence of Christmas baptism or Easter
Into the awareness of the Experiments
   and Experience of politics (and RD Laing's putative bird of paradise)
Even then...

(beyond no *great Expectations of that Charles Dickens*
Beyond David Copperfield' and his glass of Stella
 And his auntie-psychiatry with RD Laing and Thomas Szasz)
Beyond imagination

Deeper, deep into the silence of the void
Beyond which there is ...nothing
Behind which there is ... nothing

Beware of remembering.... nothing
Beware the void...
Arbeit Macht Frei?

Potential

Clare College knowledge of
 Dorset Hardy's erstwhile cottage
(Hollyhocks high in the evening sky)
Dreaming spires as buzzing bees fly by
Angels singing glory hallelujahs
Within their New Orleans sized cars
Angers dispersed from here to Tangiers
Turning humanity away from tears and fears
All the world is staged side by sides
As the riverside eyes focus on the rising tides
This *summa* the Christ's Mass
Seems overturned by the latest forecast Prophet
(No-one by violence will enter the Kingdom of Heaven)
Hannibal's long day's journey into the night of Rome
In order to assimilate all its mighty profit
The rising yeast prods the bread unleavened
Empowering our lots of salt to strike for Home
In order to discover our inner spirit and all its genius, specious class
That everyone is 'goodenough' and All should Peter's examination pass

Material Science

19 02 07

The Rev James McNaughtie
In his collars and his cuffs
Rapidly reaching forty
Avoids appearing tough
But in his youth he ran the mile
In three minutes forty five
Always greeting people ready with a smile
But when he was only twenty one
He let his motor do a ton
And more's the point he's still alive
Before the rising sun...

Washing out his weekly font
He doesn't mind the fun
That young folk have (as is their wont)
Cos like Augustine way back when
He'd rather preach God's love than Zen...

Growing up East-ender
Every moment is as tender
As the first time God touched
His quite athletic, soulful heart:
His philosophy un-couched
By neither lace nor gin in part
Almost like *Santiago*, covering all our sins
Forgiving humanity's very laden 'bins',
Bursting with morbidity and madness,
Full of the sins of sadness
And the howlings of despair...

Professing faith's real philosophy of love and daily care
Remembering when he was only ten
He abseiled off 'Big Ben'...
True man and real *Superman*
In echoes long in Mid-days shadows
Of Christ's life as carpenter
And friend of foe and fisherman

Inspired him the sacred guild of Cloth to enter
And every day one hundred times
He *swims and prays* forgiveness
For humanity's sins and crimes
Lest we forget that *Loving* was His business

In the Spirit of friendship
(and the fellowship of the Holy Spirit)

May 2006

Making space, even inner space
For friends or fellowship
Space girls, spice girls, spies, grills,
Paranoia hit the streets in Gabbatha
Un altro spavimento in Gerusalemme
Spice the final frontier
'Cold common sense and fur'
(Take 1000mg Vitamin C)
In place of Gold, frankincense and myrrh...

Spice: the plural of spouse,
For this *Scouse-Git* cath'lic philosopher
'til death us do part'
Dextrously weeding the mustard cress
Arabidopsis thaliana
From his garden path...

Ye Gods and denizens! Good Queen Bess!
Not even Torquimada expected the inquisition
Into Christian purity once the Moors left Spain:
'but a job is a job' Torqui said
As I learnt once in the Department of Anatomy
' *plus Don't we all smell as sweet*
At the headstone' – he added somewhat sinisterly ...
Coughing and Choking on the formalin in the air...

Be it the Ciskei or Transkei
or e'en the Orange Free State...
(Where enslavement of the spirit is not unknown)
'Bless your little cotton socks Kunta-kinti ' someone added,
From the wings where the angels cry
And whence the rain falls...
And the sun doth shine on occasion...
Thank God for Jesus
But don't forget to pray

...BEGINNINGS AND ENDINGS...

Fruit

c1998

If faith determines all our paths
And even colours fix our life
Painting is not without meaning
A Jaffa-esque fruit plucked fresh from plant green leaf
Causes no more consternation
Than it should...

Pluck this green naïf from all around the Durban's orange coast
And love's long journey will defend itself in kind,
Contravene the hidden law
And hope itself dissipates:
Life shrivels
While pipped Hope's rind
Eats up something
Beyond its own time...

autism?

Dec 2005

Between the braggadocio of youth
And this asinine nature of old age
Lies the concept 'liquidity';

Between the Jesuitic fingers
And the docile lips of communion
Is the space between words;

Between the sorrow'd tear
And the discovery of Light
Is the cost of loving;

Between the expectation and the reality:
'MIND THE GAP',
mind the gap...

'twixt disembarking and alighting:
 mined :the Gap

Walls and Bridges

Spring 2006

The Vine Bridge that connected like to like
    was suspended
                Between Snow's choice two cultures:
                Science *or* Humanity...
Love of Life or a life of love
Like the tenuous link,
             that sparse geometric construct
That is St John's Mathematical Bridge at Cambridge
Across a river flowing into the midnight moonlight
I and many others now can walk across that water as though on faith ...

As you would a conduit fashioned in the jungles of the Far East Sumatran forest
I would not look down lest this bird in flight might take fright and fall to earth ...
Sparse but sufficient unto the day trip from Oxford,
Hung like a fear of disconnection in the air
Unlike the heavy shaped Bridge of Sighs modelled
On the Rialto *originale* in Venice...

 Reconstructing the Bridge of Mostar linking
Former Jugoslavian Muslim
                       with former Jugoslavian Christian
Connecting Tennyson's feeling words
        With
            Rossetti's
               Angelic
                    pre-lapsarian
                          Pre-Raphaelites
Now Coming down to earth,
              hear,
                from heav'ns magnanimous heights
this deep and real connection, bears a light across a cultural division...

Peering into Rebecca's well
                              Both yesterday as today
Then turning with *Adam* (east of Eden) to teach tomorrow

Hanging in mid thought
                              The sparse bridge gives way
Suddenly it's day...

Malheureusement la morbidite' ne respecte pas personne position ou temps

Hanging on for dear life the judger himself finds his own survivor's path
Adjudged and unabridged
        So waiting for his returning native wit,
                a surging life wish inherent in us all
    Encouraged and awash with angels
        he finds himself miraculously germane,
                                        unharmed ....

That tenuous arching spiral link that over vaults
                              its mathematical purity
Conjoins us to life and matter in the inherent symmetry

                              of the DNA
That binds the angels and the spirit to this o'er populous
                              earthen birth
And makes us all appreciate God's own and special new aesthetic
                in the beauty of His created double helix spiral
                                        (just don't forget it)
    As you pray and hand across your money
    This precision aspect of God's Law
    Has the satisfaction of discovering in us
    The elegance of Nature's secret harmony
    In the equation of the music of the spheres
    Which moves in both a limnology of feelings
    And the moonlight neap tide of memory, dreams, reflection
    Both Jung and old alike
    On a bridge at midnight observing
    The soul and the spirit and the marrow...

Life has an obligation to appear
To obey that law of love...
Without the need for Christian's Christmas cash-till 'kerchings!'
   And all those other seasonal glitzy ersatz things...
To save each and every humanity
                    from a genetic programmed
                                        pre lapsarian fall from Grace...?
Or even remind us of our washed away iniquity?
And that the music of heaven's spheres we should face
And deeply humbly and with love embrace?

Trivial Pursuits

Sunday 19/02/06

Jason and his thousand screaming Argonauts
Fleeced his imagery till it bled
Us clean (and since it had its trivial pursuits in ancient texts)
An angel of mercy stoops to help a human path,
As when we stumble and someone helps us cross
The road that leads on up to deeper things
(An awareness of beyond the 'hear and now')
Appears and aids us on our way...
As they slip off with our wallet, keys and pocket-watch

Global Warning

17 03 06

Global Warming is such a threat
With all the generals leaders politicians too
Talking so much hot air they create but bet
They know the panacea of all ills
Ignoring the elder wise men who
With insight wisdom and assorted skills
Claim arcane knowledge of humanity
And are surely able to stave off this calamity
Jain, Christian Hindu,
 Sikh, Muslim, Jew
All talking against each other but with hearing weak
Not listening nor receiving always speaking and expounding
(Nor yet is man able to digest philosophy resounding)
Meanwhile as our earth is measured up for global warming
Today is springtime and we have seventeen Snow-warnings...!

Garden Reverie

2002

Hollyhock high midday upright in the bending sun
The garden soothes with warmth
Heavy, laden bumbles buzzing
                              bullying the fragrantly stigmatised pollen petals;
Appearing as disturbance between dimensions
Trailing a cloak of pollen conquest behind
Seeking new financial honey pots above them
Stirring the reveries of filmic assonance inside a quiet garden dream world
With the intimations of externalities beyond these walls

Busy, busy, busy then away...
Glistening water-sounds washing and
                    Allaying our iniquities behind us
Flowing as constant as circular logic saws grinding through some bark
The rustle in the leaves, moving the air
Heavy with summer song
The door bell rings and now
 We are awake 'ere long...

Amethyst Heaven

24 II 06

Under the evening Amethyst Sky
I watch the last of summer's flowers
 After the night times storm windily shake their selves dry
Earthly life and humanity's various powers
 Intertwine as richly as the electric chords
My daughter strums on her guitar
 Echo round the Spirit that they afford spirit's passage
Through our own and our neighbours' houses
 Here I write, quiet as a church mouse's
Rememberings of today: a family of nieces, nephews
                          (and their growth spurts and catarrh...)
 Having seen my dad 'doddery' catch himself
Before he fell, as I watered our departed *mama's* African violets on their shelf
 I reflect upon the violet amethyst sky,
Feeling good but mellow if not necessarily 'high'
 I watch crepuscular amethyst *'entre chien et loup'*
Gown itself in the darker shades of its night time troop
 As night descends to guard us in our sleep
The love of God I pray in your heart us to keep...
Our life within this world, too, see us through.

Midnight at the Oasis of the Insomniac

7th July 2006

Instead of a heavy dark midnight, a foreboding gloomily retold
My head one cold December night at college
(having witnessed a mis -toiled forceps, subsequent loss, lost blood)
Exploded out into one hundred thousand milk white butterflies
Which live here still in a corner of my dank and musty mind
Leaving me speechless and without breath...
And one year closer to ...
Occasionally when I wake up to the day from that corner of that long
       forgotten memory
I flutter like a thousand disparate inchoate thoughts arching up to sunny sky
And being a gentle soul at heart they do not tangle with the webs and threads
I let them be and do not wave a broom or strike a stick at fluttered
       'wings' again...

And then my Father does not call me in to see him to reproach me
Nor tick me off nor wag his finger at me in disappointment and some pain...

Every Little Dream...

C. 2000

In inverse proportion to my fear
The base of my house appears to disappear
Though *Giordano Bruno* is renowned
For fiscal prudence he wears a frown
(a prudent man is happier with a frown)
The house we live in, the roof, the walls
The independent company that weathers squalls
Is battened down to resist a storm
To push ahead from trough to crest as though a norm
Of expectation had been now addressed
The waves are rough and the sea is cruel
Our children Adam and Rebecca
Asleep upstairs: they need a chance.
But the ship and sea these two must duel
This rhyme is not first-perfect
And this ignorance is not my last
But the words I write I hear are from my heart
Till tempest cast is tempest past.
And economic waves are calmed and draining off the deck
And sea-calm sea relives the dawn
That lights the house that's built upon a rock
And though the night be cold
And freezing rain makes all feel old
The light of lights appear to shock
The patient unto a cough
                        and mourn
The passing of the night
                        And light upon us shine
As though the rain itself were
                        Now turned wine
And day was new begun...

Blackcurrant Sorbet Geode:
($e^{\pi i} + 1 = 0$)

On my daughter's 10th Birthday
22-10-06

Should my reach exceed my grasp (or what's a heaven for?)
And I could not hear Auden's sorry phrase
('...drug as they may the Sybils utter a gush of table chat...')
And I reflect not, before sleep, on topaz of Ethiope nor peridot nor chrysoprase...
If looking through the soft focus pink stone lens door
Of perception and any or all of that
(The sound of suffering jazz snaking round the midnight foggy lamp post)
What good does it afford my self,
To wish upon a star for health?
What is worse to dream to want to walk on water
Or being serious tread carefully on dreams of skating hoar-frost Ice?
(Especially as life ain't always as it oughta)
Light and lenses crystal reflect back to us our Divine Host
With love light to show humanity the way:
                      and ain't that cool and just and NICE?
God's construction defines our Nature's formulae and Laws
(But also limits us to our human flaws
So we do not fly like angels aethereal
And needs must before Our Own Creator kneel)
Light through lenses crystal show humanity, Joy is real
Glimpsed here through Revelation's Seal:
My wife and family and friends My Son and Daughter my own hope do heal...

Light

Friday 13th October 2006

Light is understanding that light perseveres through heavy periods
Periods that light the way like heavy rain watering the harvest yet to be,
   'The life of the world to come'
Light is communion, structured for prayer as for telepathy
At oneness, and one, a Kantian thought in itself...
(Feeling-at –a – distance like quarks separate
 At their moment of conception 'In the Mind's Eye')...
Separate coherent conjoined 'entanglement'
Separate by identified identical paths
Through a faith in science
Light is a metaphor for thought
Nothing travels faster than light
Nothing can be conceptualised that travels
   Faster than the ability to conceptualise
      (a pre-Copernican stance?)
Thought opens the door to love
Yet love opens the door to thought
Love is not a word any more than *God* is a three letter word
Love is a painful Calvary which God only knows
      we probably don't deserve...
And yet almost as the biological imperative of the desire to procreate
Are we taken by the hand to the very threshold of understanding
To which every mortal sentient aspires
     In order to reach out to a higher state of being...
(What's a heaven for if mere mortals can grasp the concept in a phrase?)
Reaching out for God, standing in the need of God's Love (because
   God is Loving)
 Loving will make any burden Light...
       Even a cross.

So light is understanding
Even the heaviness of a cross
Across the loss across the eyes...

Thoughts, Memories, Dreams, Reflections:

- 'Closure of The Ospedale Italiano,

Queen Square, London' (1980 Newspaper headline)

LH
Autumn 1996

Between the bread of the presence of mind
And the blood
      Of the absence of conflict
Whole golf swings of missed opportunities
Which don't interrupt the Sunday afternoon mood
Where each hour may indeed last a thousand years

And a few minutes in the Dean's Office somebody's lifetime

But out there in casualty
Where the truth may be in waiting
Each lifetime may be spent just in the closing of a curtain
And each thousandth year marked
By the ticking numbers in a queuing system
Where nobody is and nobody wants to be
But where Aneurin's black-dog poodle spins
Quietly in its electron orbit of *some or other* grave
               of gravest syndromes...

While Sister hunts out aspirin
The financial headaches persevere...
Again the NHS is in a spin
Wherein good old Barts. begets its spirit,(good Rahere)
To give the Foreigner as well his due
Holds close those valued principles warm, m'dear
To help tomorrow
 And tomorrow and tomorrow.

Under the Green Light of a Crescent Moon
(...A green thought in a green shade...)

23-11-05

If I go into the darkness tonight
Then I will be alone without reason
If I go out into the fog without light
My reason will take flight in or out of season
If in boxing up my shadows sitting on the cliff
Wishing I could translate my pain into a saxophone riff
I would teeter on the eve of my mother's birthday
Before an alighting butterfly turns even my gloomy joy into quiet mirth today
To let me edge or walk away ... should I choose to stay.

So I went out (*'force majeure'*) into that Good night
Sky as deep as silk peppered with pointed light
First for my daughter with her *'petits verres'*
And friends in a Brownie pack and embarrassed laughter
Then for my son for his 'St John's' in uniform (all shiny shoes and shiny hair).

Racing round like a pigeon to chase after
The hiring of the hall for this weekend –the family gathering
To celebrate a good person's 'joie de vivre' and good-life
Some-one's sister, some-one's daughter, our mother,
                                        my father's friend and wife
One of the many that had taught me parenthood, even into my own fathering.

Immured

Rome 2005
at my mother's grave
where mortal remains are lain to rest
within a village of houses of walls of tombs
and where there is a bus stop...

Within that walled necropolis
An end of time: to us the end of childhood
Forever, and a day and today that strange day
where life and death briefly kiss

Where once a fighting spirit stood
There is emptiness of the tomb
Whatever you say no one understood
That human life had come to this

Even when the auto bus stops en route
And my turn is here today
Who will welcome the sentient
Who will comfort the grieving
Who will acknowledge
that this is only a beginning
In love and prayer ...

Crossing Styx

6/10/05

I AM that lost soul on the Ship Nirvana
Between the hear and now
        Between the broken kiss of holy bread
And the cracked lips neath furrowed brow
Receiving the love of Christ in faith...

I am embroiled 'neath both skull cap and bandana
In those racing thoughts, borne to us as children of sorrow
              And Resurrection
And, I hear, in the sighing of frustration,
           (wishing to howl at the moon)
Standing in the need of Love and God
        Hearing only reproof and correction...
I am tied to gravity's rainbow
        Tethered to white light
(some-one using the Hand cuffs of guilt?)

Unable to fly released
I am Tithed to purgatory
           Till morning come
And the angel of god be pleased.

Healing

After discovering the John Lennon
Platinum discs in a café
along the Kings Road, London.
April 2006

As the water flows in the pocket sized garden of Eden
And the rustling leaves have even less to do with Abba, Father
(and even less with far off Sweden home of the Volvo)
Herein the anaesthetic talk of Indian deities
Of many arms and many warned
Subsumed into the sentience and the conscious and the prescience of the other
 And the open door appears at Source without apparent cause
The wrong word said and hereinafter mourned
While Adam draws near his sense of sauce,
'*Logogenesis*' wholly spirit draws in near
(And the force of reason of course)
Pursues its trivial purgatorial circles of language, truth and logic and the fear
That my son (his broken arm and a few lost stones)
Listens as the Sybil her teaching to him intones.
And begins to Adam and Eve in life...

House and Home

For our mother Carmela Concetta Hill (née Sciuto-Sturzo)
Born 26:11:24 + died 30:6:05

1)House

La mamma Roma

3/7/05

La Mama Roma è eterna
La mamma Roma sarà
Domani come era ieri

Oggi la mamma Roma è quieta
Sotto il cielo azurro
Tranquillo senza perturbo
La mamma Roma beata
Conosce tutto,sappià tutto
Perdona tutto...

Ringraziamo Gesù Cristo
Per la vita
Della Mamma Roma
Città Eterna...

11) Home

Mother Rome is eternal
Mother Rome will be
Tomorrow as was yesterday...
Today Mother Rome is quietly
Resting under an azure sky
Tranquil and undisturbed.
Beautiful Mother Rome
Believes everything, knows everything
Forgives everything...
Let us all thank the Lord, Jesus Christ
For the Life of Our dear Mother Rome
Eternal City and now Eternal Mother...

Where the Sun Shines
(you Don't Always Feel the Cold)

13-3-06

When the sun is shining, life can seem most pleasing.
Looking out across the park from Richmond's Pembroke Lodge
Without the fear that my function is mere appeasing
(*Medicus enim nihil aliud est quam animae consolatio*),
is to quote Petronius
And that real life and reality I shouldst not dodge
Where the drink at the 'Son and Dove', Denmark Hill, is just a bonus.

I sit and write and watch the busy day go by-
It should be spring, a cold spring, midway through Lent
Waiting for goodwill to appear to tap my shoulder and say 'Hi'
I write as though disconnected from my concerns of where my life went

I sit, in a car, over looking the park road traffic
Thinking on how a good life can also be magic
Appreciating that some things are from God (and therefore heaven sent)
I listen to the Mozart clarinet larghetto music disc
Remembering how when the sun shines life can be most pleasing...
Even if quite frankly the weather really is quite freezing.

Encounter

25 01 07
(Burns night)

At Adam Pond, Richmond park
I walk around the long circumference
In the chill post snow air, fingers bitten by the wind...
My intention? To throw some stones into the middle
To make a splash, cause some ripples
(as suggested: to release summed feeling)...
But then I think how at its centre is an island dealing,
Like a Van Gough chair, of deepest feeling
That in my mind I keep occasioning to *chance* upon at every other minute
That when I am in meditation I revere it as some inspired source
Of Knowledge or of Wisdom and Respect. That some regret.
So because I live as a green thought in a green shade in a glass greenhouse
I *choose* that I do not throw a stone (lest some stones be thrown back)
Instead I should walk around frustrated anger as I do this pond
In 'la belle sighs park'
And now I am free
 and definitely overworked
I ask
 How could I for one stupid moment have confused it with myself?
And the morning answers to me through silence in the wind.

I walk around, to watch the moor hens and the ducks and geese
Because I cannot walk on water (even if so frozen thin)
Right round to where a little tributary bleeds
Across the edge and over
Into a rivulet that forms a cross of irrigation for the field.

Further round I walk
Around a bench mark where a pair of child sized gloves lie
        discarded and soaked into the melting snow

Just then
Two beautiful white swans, mated for life, glide serenely by
I walk round a little further and look across:

There upon a bower rising as a crescent from the water
Seven white seagulls perching equidistant
As though a choir of angels had descended
To this earth to re-witness a new birth...
I sit down again   to write a song
(and right a wrong along the way)
Two women, one black, one white
Offer salutation as they walk on apace
'Drawing?' one asks 'No writing' I reply
'Have a good day' they say
So I take out my camera to photograph
A sun ray burst flowing from a window in the cloud...

The Shock of the News

1997

Once upon a time (a very long time ago now)
I witnessed a patient become clamped against his bed
To await his own arc of electric light medicine
That while I watched the switch was flicked
And current values surged throughout him
To seek out the tracts that caused dismay
Sin-burnt skin to unforgiving sin within
So I observed, learning nothing 'cept this fear
As my patient arched convulsively
Jerking bitterly before finally sleeping out his longer day..

So now all humanity washed clean
(The doctors moved on up to higher things)
Patient and shaman absolved of memories
That I would say *if I should voice for him*
His feelings of reaction from the grey
'Thank you this had worked quite well'
Indeed I and my assailant might converse

I might thank him for his time
And not complain to him about Amnesia
If I should remember, since the seizure
Nor remember that I growled when angry
(so much more often than I used to)
And as for those spots afore my eyes
Well I would have ventured nothing 'rash'
In case it aggravated my new and nervous 'tic'

So as the great Professor's Aides attend and students learn
(all to discover their own Truth in waiting)
I would sit and shiver out the cold of Life
Before this mouse should drop to floor of house
Amidst the littered cups Pierian (their contents now all quaffed)
From whence these shallowed draughts intoxicated
Had I learned, but only dangerously just sipped:
Nor had I imbibed so deeply, nor enough...

Bitter Medicine

LH
24th March 2007

One Sunday coming home along the motorway from Cardiff Bay
Driving along Society's
Displaced discarded jetsam
Caused no doubt by
Bad Advice *'discard if difficult'*
Discard if bad news becomes
Bad Medicine immediately expressed...

No breakdown in justice?
(What if...? Aah well never mind...)
Oh you know just accept the delayed *giustizia-*
As if *giustizia* delayed is not *giustizia* denied
Count yourself in, (one two, three, four, and five...)
Another car overtakes and another
Freewill.co.uk –what do you think?
 What thoughts (if any)?

Should someone, anyone, be allowed to drive along the motorway
          single handedly
(With a baby child in the back) uncontrollably moving his left hand
In swirling curling athetoid movements?
(Because he can you know ....)

Or was he conducting an orchestra on the radio with his one good free hand
And I had misperceived him ...?

About The Author

Lewis Hill was educated at St Benedict's, Ealing in West London where he received a well rounded education and developed a sense of humour. He went up to London University in the mid seventies to pursue a course of medical training at St Mary's Hospital. This education as a doctor exposed him to the variety of the 'human condition' that both challenged and deepened his appreciation of the spiritual aspects of life. It was here that he first realized that human nature is always standing in the need of God. He then went on to take a Masters in Psychology which gave him the excuse to peruse the pages of Freud, Jung, Adler and Catullus.

Having studied the likes of Lucretius (for its poetry) and Russell, Hume, Paine and Locke (for their enlightenment) he developed an interest in the impact the environment (both internal and external) plays in human behaviour.

In the mid 80s he had several short stories broadcast on a London-wide talk-based radio. More recently in the 90s he has contributed to five anthologies of poetry, (receiving a commendation for one contribution).

His writing has also featured in magazines and in-house journals. This is his first book of collected works.

He has worked as a counsellor for Victim Support for twelve years, helping clients recover from the aftermath of crimes.

A tireless fundraiser for Cancer Research he has completed numerous cycle marathons around London, abseiled off a Crystal Palace tower block and accomplished a 'commando slide' from the top of Twickenham stadium. He has even spent a night in Wormwood Scrubs in 2005 to raise funds for this worthwhile charity.

He is married to Fiona by whom he has two children, Adam and Rebecca, and still lives in Ealing, London.

Printed in the United Kingdom
by Lightning Source UK Ltd.
121174UK00001B/381